MW01181855

Fellow Dreamers

Oklahoma, Education and the World

Paul William Bass

Paul Bass 10/25/08

NEW FORUMS
Stillwater, Oklahoma
U.S.A.

NEW FORUMS PRESS

Produced in the United States of America
by New Forums Press, 1018 S. Lewis St.
Stillwater, OK 74074
www.newforums.com

Copyright © 2008 by Paul William Bass.

All rights reserved. No part of this publication may be reproduced or
transmitted in any form or by any means, electronic or mechanical,
including photocopy, or any information storage or retrieval system,
without permission in writing from the publisher.

Library of Congress Cataloging-in-Publication Data Pending

Printed in the United States of America.

ISBN 10: 1-58107-145-0
ISBN 13: 978-1-581071-45-0

Contents

Author's Notes

In my first book, *No Little Dreams*, a biography of Henry Garland Bennett, I closely followed Bennett's background and accomplishments, highlighting encounters with his "fellow dreamers," yet treating them peripherally. In this book, I have brought to center stage the interrelationships among Bennett and his contemporaries, for certainly one man's successes happen in tandem from the influence of other great men. Rethinking the impact of Bennett as a collaborative success, I have come to see the timeliness of this new approach.

Following the publication in 2007 of *No Little Dreams*, a number of key events have confirmed that Bennett figures largely in American history because he never appears alone. This is first evident in the wide influence of the whole Bennett family. On March 2, 2007, over 60 Bennett family members, from fourteen states, gathered at Ouachita Baptist University in Arkadelphia, Arkansas, in celebration of the centennial of Bennett's college graduation, a governor's proclamation honoring Henry Garland Bennett was being given to the family and a debate/speech scholarship established on the Ouachita Baptist University campus in Bennett's honor. On April 13, 2007, a permanent display honoring Bennett was dedicated in the Oklahoma History Center in Oklahoma City, Oklahoma, Bennett family members were being recognized and honored at that event. On December 14, 2007, when I was honored with the Henry G. Bennett Distinguished Fellow Award from the School of International Studies at Oklahoma State University in Stillwater, Oklahoma, there by my side was Thomas Edwin Bennett, Bennett's youngest and only surviving child, being given an honorary Bennett Fellow award. The second evidence that Bennett's importance is not isolated is that his pattern of influence seems to be repeating itself in our day. As during the Cold War when Bennett created new collaborative efforts to responsibly share the success of Americans in order to alleviate poverty in the world, now advancing organizations such as the Carter Center, Heifer International, Doctors Without

Borders, the Clinton Global Consortium, the Bill and Linda Gates Foundation, and other responsible, religious international relief programs, continue to combine personal compassion with political savvy. None of these organizations do so single handedly. As Bennett was a team player with William Holloway, Robert Kerr, Harry Truman, Haile Selassie, Benjamin Hardy and James Webb, so, too, the approach for change seems democratic. It is the esprit de corps of these "fellow dreamers" that this book unfolds.

In the research for this book, I was very aware of Oklahoma's Centennial celebration and the great impact that these individuals had in the state. Sadly, no biographies have been written on the individual lives of most of these significant "fellow dreamers." I was very fortunate to have contact with immediate family members, many aging, of some of these men who provided personal accounts and valuable research materials. Family members have been gracious with their encouragement and approval, even proofing the related chapters. I am indebted to them and hope that this book will provide an important, lasting record of these men and their collaborative efforts in fulfilling their dreams—personal, national and even international.

About the Author

Paul William Bass is the former director of campus activities and the debate coach for Ouachita Baptist University in Arkadelphia, Arkansas. He lives there with his wife Jan. Born in Independence, Missouri, he has served at Ouachita since 1990. Previously, a full-time staff member in churches in Arkansas, Alabama and Missouri, he is currently pastor of the Anchor Baptist Church in Brown Springs, Arkansas

Other books he has authored are *The World Traveler's Companion: A Handbook for Group Trip Leaders*, *In Jesus' Names*, *Minor Characters of the Bible*, and *A History of Debate at Ouachita Baptist University*.

Foreword

Henry Garland Bennett was an individual who loomed larger than life in many circles— most notably higher education in Oklahoma. Though he tragically died more than fifty years ago in the service of his country, Dr. Bennett is still highly regarded in Oklahoma.

In *No Little Dreams*, author Paul Bass rekindled the life of Henry Bennett and his service to his community, state and nation. However, one volume was not enough to tell of Bennett's relationships with important state, national and international political leaders. With *Fellow Dreamers*, Bass continues the story of Bennett's distinguished career and friendships that developed over his life. Such notables of Oklahoma history include Governors William Holloway and Robert S. Kerr who later rose to serve in the United States Senate; both were lifelong friends who provided opportunities by introducing Bennett to James Webb and subsequently President Harry S. Truman.

Henry G. Bennett was not a native-born Oklahoman, yet his imprint on Oklahoma is vast and continues to influence generations today through his service to his country and his appointment as director of the Point Four program that ultimately led to his meeting international figures of prominence in their day. All of these connections tell a story of Bennett and his *Fellow Dreamers*.

William D. Welge, CA
Director
Research Division
Oklahoma Historical Society
June, 2008

This book is dedicated to the memory of

Francis Elizabeth Corbin Bennett,

extraordinary person, dear friend and great encourager. She was the wife of Phil Connell Bennett, second son of Henry and Vera Bennett. She died in a tragic accident on August 17, 2007, at the age of 91.

"Snooks"

Introduction

As Oklahoma celebrated its state centennial, an interconnected group of fellow dreamers was discovered. Though the connecting thread among these fellow dreamers is Henry Garland Bennett, his impact on Oklahoma education and politics in the first half century of Oklahoma's statehood still being felt to this day, this Arkansas-born dreamer had a profound national and international impact because he united with other dreamers.

In Philip Rulon's *History of Oklahoma State University* one paragraph provided the motivation to examine the lives of these men who in collaborative support accomplished great deeds:

> Robert Kerr and Henry Bennett had much in common. Both had been born in a log cabin, had been reared in the Southwest and lived in Little Dixie, had attended the University of Oklahoma, and had been pillars in the Baptist Church. Then, too, William J. Holloway had given each of them their initial push upwards. He had worked for Bennett's appointment to head the land-grant college and had chosen Kerr to replace J. W. Clark as a special justice of the Oklahoma Supreme Court... Kerr and Bennett remained close for the rest of their lives. They seldom failed to consult with each other on important matters. When, for example, Kerr accepted an invitation to deliver the keynote speech at the National Democratic Convention in 1944 at Chicago, Bennett helped him draft the message.

This passage shows the interrelationship that Henry Bennett had with "fellow dreamers" to accomplish great things for the university, the state, nation and many foreign countries. Others whose interrelationships followed along the lines of those above were Harry S. Truman, Emperor Haile Selaisie, Benjamin H. Hardy, and James E. Webb. Among these distinguished gentlemen would be found public school teachers, a college president, state representatives, state senators, governors, state department leaders, military aides, an emperor, a vice-president and president. They were all men of different backgrounds and different career paths, but they were all commoners with an understanding of human needs and dignity. All were well-educated men, except for Truman who was unable to attend college. All served in the military except for Bennett who worked to provide for education for thousands of veterans. The one thing unifying all of these men was their direct association with Henry Bennett and the commonality of their dreams for the improvement of the plight of mankind, nationally and internationally.

The programs Dr. Bennett helped to establish are not only being historically documented, but are also continuing and expanding through the Oklahoma State University International Education and Outreach Program and the United States Agency for International Development (USAID) program. The impact of the other men continues to be felt today in state, national and international agencies. The activities of these men have often been lost to immediate family memories and occasional, historical references. Bennett and his contemporaries faced national and international challenges that are similar to those of today. Underdeveloped countries continue to suffer from the devastation of war and entire populations of people face starvation and genocide. Corrupt rulers and totalitarian regimes continue to thwart the efforts of assistance and progress within their countries. The advances of modern technology in education, agriculture, disease control, and construction have vastly improved since Bennett's time, but still remain out of reach to most of the world's population. With an increase in the number of effective, non-government organizations whose leaders share the dreams of Henry Bennett, perhaps an interrelationship with today's "fellow dreamers" can accomplish much beyond Bennett's great dreams for an equally needy world.

Chapter One

Henry Garland Bennett

A man of "no little dreams"

Not only did Henry Garland Bennett have the fortune of being born into a family of dreamers, but he was able to marry a dreamer and then cross paths with fellow dreamers throughout his career. He is one of the threads of commonality between the other men. Their mutual collaboration was made possible by belief in the ability to better humankind. Two of these men—Bennett and Hardy— would lose their lives on foreign soil in the direct effort to accomplish their dreams. After their untimely deaths in 1951, Henry Bennett and Benjamin Hardy had left well-established families that produced many dreamers who are continuing to follow their example.

Background of a Dreamer

Henry's ancestors came with big dreams and big risks to Arkansas from North Carolina and Tennessee when Arkansas was still Indian Territory. Arkansas became a state in 1836. With the interruption of the Civil War, they became very successful homesteaders in the mid-1800s. The simplicity of the term "homesteader" was not representative of the big dreams, risks and hard work needed to claim that title. The Bennetts settled around Hope, Arkansas, working the land, establishing families and meeting the requirements for land ownership. They were a close family, religious and industrious. Henry's great-grandfather was Richard Allen Bennett. His grandfather was George Washington Bennett. His father was Thomas Jefferson Bennett. Thomas Jefferson married Mary Elizabeth Bright December 3, 1879. They gave birth to two daughters, Mary Stella and Lois. Henry Garland Bennett was born December 14, 1886.

Henry Bennett's father, Thomas Jefferson Bennett, was a farmer/ evangelist who was nearly blind, but the handicap failed to discourage his continued dreams for his family. After Henry was born the family made an attempt to live in East Texas before settling back in Arkansas. Several of the Bennett family members were also evangelists who were attending the newly-established Ouachita College in Arkadelphia, Arkansas. Influenced by those experiences and dreaming of a college education for their children, Thomas and Mary moved their family to Arkadelphia in 1895. They built a boarding house with lumber from their homestead farmland. The boarding house provided family income and an opportunity for boarding college faculty who, in turn, would tutor the Bennett children to help them prepare for college classes. This also allowed Thomas to continue his evangelistic travel.

Preparing for the Dreams

Fulfilling dreams is hard work and often requires the assistance of fellow dreamers. Henry attended the primary school program at Ouachita College. As a child he met and established a lifelong friendship with William Judson Holloway. Henry helped at the boarding house with gardening, laundry, cleaning and cooking. He was also industrious in holding several responsible jobs. He provided a laundry pick up and delivery service for a local cleaner. He delivered groceries by wagon. At age sixteen he became the first rural delivery postman in Arkansas. He delivered mail by horseback on horses provided by his grandfather, George Washington Bennett, who had also moved to Arkadelphia.

Early in his life Henry had established the ability and willingness to work hard to accomplish his personal dreams. Henry entered Ouachita College classes in 1905. Because of his earlier tutoring he was able to complete his college education in two years. He was active on the college campus in sports, debating and publications. He graduated in 1907 with a bachelor of arts degree. During the summers in college Henry found time to sell books. He traveled to Oklahoma (then still Indian Territory) and Kansas and was successful in his sales efforts. He was also able to establish his own library of great literature. After college graduation, Bennett taught in a private business school in Texarkana. When the school failed financially, Bennett went back to selling books. On one of his trips to Oklahoma, he found an employment opportunity in the small town of Boswell. Oklahoma had become a state that fall of 1907 and getting trained teachers to come to the former Indian Territory was difficult. Bennett accepted a teaching/superintendent position in Boswell. He was instrumental in getting several Ouachita College graduates to come to his district and teach. One was his friend William Holloway. Bennett was offered and accepted the position of Choctaw County superintendent in 1909. He interviewed and hired new teachers. One of these was Vera Pearl Connell, who would later become Mrs. Henry Bennett.

While in Hugo, Bennett would become involved with the Southeastern State Normal School (SEN) in Durant, Oklahoma. He attended several classes and then was asked to teach summer classes. He became an active proponent of teachers completing and continuing their education—especially at the Durant school. Bennett would complete his master's degree from the University of Oklahoma in 1924 by attending summer classes. He would go on to complete his Ph.D. in one year at Columbia University in New York City in 1926. His Ph.D. work, calling for the creation of a state constitutional coordinating board, would later provide the basis for the structure of higher education for the state of Oklahoma.

Bennett's period of courtship with Vera Pearl Connell would prove to be mutually challenging. She was also born in Arkansas, in Conway, and moved with her family to Durant, Oklahoma in 1897. Each had their personal and professional dreams. It was probably more difficult at that time period for Vera. Women's rights and professional status were yet to be recognized. Finally on January 27, 1913, Henry and Vera were married in her father's home in Durant.

Bennett continued at Hugo but grew in his attachment to the Durant school. He and Vera began a family which grew to have three children: Henry, Jr.; Phil and Liberty. In the spring of 1919, Bennett was offered and accepted the position of president of the Southeastern State Normal School. He and Vera moved their family to Durant that summer as he began his official duties. It became a pattern that several families and friends would follow the Bennetts from Hugo to Durant. Henry set out to accomplish the tasks of developing a faithful faculty and staff and serving the needs of teachers in the state. He was also very conscious of the need to establish good community relationships with the school in a philosophy of action that he called "Town and Gown." In the fall of 1919 Bennett led the community in hosting the Southeastern Oklahoma Education Association's annual two-day meeting. They returned the next year which added significant income to the entire community. In the winter of 1919, the United Mine Workers of America had threatened a nationwide strike that would have created a shortage of coal for the Durant community. The local newspaper reported that "Bennett personally led 100 men from the campus to the woods to provide heating fuel for the relief of the community." He also became active in community improvements, such as streets and sidewalks, which also helped the campus in its physical development. As the school grew in numbers, causing increased housing needs, Henry coordinated with families in the community for students to work in exchange for room and board. Henry and Vera were also active in student/community employment needs. Henry also found time to join the charter membership of the Rotary International in Durant in the mid-1920s. He would be an active member for the rest of his life, even becoming the president of the 12th District of Rotary International in Oklahoma.

Bennett's hard work was now being channeled to assist others in pursuing their dreams. Bennett led the small school into significant growth in his nine years in Durant. He encouraged faculty to take sabbatical leave to earn advanced degrees. Henry led in the establishment of campus programs for student development. He also set up a correspondence and extension study department. In his first year as president, Henry was able to announce the expansion of the school into a four-year academic college, to be known as Southeastern Oklahoma State Teachers College (STC). Bennett added evening classes and increased the summer program in order to attract teachers. In August of 1923, the school was recognized as "the only twelve-month college in the state." Such recognition attracted national interest. That same month the United States Veterans' Bureau informed Henry that "it would send four to five hundred ex-servicemen to campus to take courses in business administration and other related vocations." Bennett also found time to write textbooks for the state schools. This provided a needed service as well as additional income. He and the entire family were active in recruiting students from Oklahoma and Arkansas. Bennett would dismiss students' concern of finances with the promise of jobs on campus or in the community. Many graduates would remember the encouragement and assistance of the Bennetts in helping them to complete educational goals and career dreams. During Bennett's nine-year service as president, the Durant school tripled its enrollment and saw many new facilities and services added to its campus.

Actualizing the Dreams

With the successes and satisfaction of seeing his dreams fulfilled in Durant, Bennett would be tested anew to take his dreams in a new direction. In the summer of 1928, Bennett was elected president of the Oklahoma A & M College in Stillwater. His reputation as an educator in the state, and his close friendship with state political powers, gave him an inside track to the position. He came to Stillwater with a phenomenal "twenty-five year plan" for the campus. It would be his guideline for physical change for the next twenty-three years of his tenure. He faced immediate challenges of traditional board interference and faculty transitions. He established approved governing procedures as president and provided faculty tenure and sabbatical leaves. He also brought several families with him from Durant to help establish a supportive staff. He effectively lobbied in Oklahoma City and Washington, D. C. for increased funding. The 1929 Great Depression hit Oklahoma and the nation hard. Henry provided the stability to keep the college active and provided the surrounding, oil-rich counties with some relief assistance. The Dust Bowl and soil erosion had created a need to preserve Oklahoma's usable farmland. Bennett's interest in agriculture led him to establish, in 1929, the Red Plains Soil and Conservation Experimental station. This was a cooperative effort with the United States Department of Agriculture and it was the first research center of its kind in the United States. Years later Bennett would lead in the creation of the Flying Farmers organization to help with soil conservation and even livestock transportation.

Bennett drew on his previous professional dreams and duplicated some of the educational programs he found at Durant. He established short courses and correspondence-extension studies that were very popular. He worked to establish campus programs for student development and community involvement. He continued his practice of actively recruiting students desiring a college education by offering campus and community jobs. To help students with financial needs, Bennett created self-help programs such as a pottery barn and agricultural productions. He created programs for community involvement such as elderly care and fire protection. Henry created specialized branches of A & M around the state.

World War II had a great impact on A & M and an opportunity for Bennett to develop a new avenue of dreams. Young men and women were drawn away for military service, including Bennett's son. The A & M campus became a training center for over 40,000 men and women in all divisions of military service. An emergency building program was set up to establish the additional housing needs. A school for WAVES (Women Accepted for Volunteer Emergency Service) was established. The end of World War II created an opportunity for Henry to establish programs for training returning veterans. The end of the war also gave him an opportunity to pursue his interest of flying. Bennett purchased surplus airplanes for campus use. Not only did he take advantage of the time-saving flights, but he led a campaign to convince his faculty and staff to take part. In 1950 American Airlines acclaimed Henry Bennett as the college president who had accumulated the most miles traveled.

Bennett left a legacy at Oklahoma A & M College of nearly completing his original "twenty-five year plan." Over the course of his twenty-three years of service as A & M president, he took a very hands-on approach in the planning and construction of all the approved facilities. His dreams for the A & M physical campus development were almost completed. Ironically, his one unfulfilled construction project was an early-American-style chapel on campus. With his personal faith and denominational involvement, it is indeed ironic that all other building projects to help educate others were a higher priority than the chapel. Even though the campus would later name a small contemporary, campus chapel after Henry and Vera Bennett, it was a far cry from the envisioned chapel that Bennett had planned.

Bennett was fortunate to have a wife who was not only supportive, but very involved in his daily activities. Each morning she had a list prepared for Bennett of things that needed to be accomplished that day. In 1920 Vera gave birth to twins, Thomas and Mary. She often had to run the household of five children alone because of Henry's travels and appointments. Both Bennett and his wife, Vera, were very active in the First Baptist Church of Stillwater. Each taught large college-age Sunday School classes, Henry the men's class and Vera the women's class. Henry was a member of the church's building committee. Both were active in the Southern Baptist state and national conventions where they assumed program leadership positions. Bennett was in demand as a lay speaker across the state.

From early in his life Bennett had established some interesting personal habits. He was a constant reader with a great ability to memorize information. He had a strange philosophy about sleep. He felt that people wasted much of their time by sleeping and could better use their time in pursuit of other activities—both academic and physical. That accounted for his ability to complete his advanced degrees so quickly. That also caused Bennett's contact with family and friends to be at rather odd hours of the night or morning. His driving across country was usually non-stop. Bennett had developed skills in public speaking from his college days. He was a debater and active in the forensics program. Those skills would bring him recognition as a good communicator and requested speaker. He could also be persuasive in communicating his dreams to others.

Bennett was very involved in politics—state and national. On the state level, he had a wonderful relationship with childhood friend William Holloway. Holloway was elected lieutenant governor and later became governor after an impeachment. His role in both offices were of help to Bennett and his career. Bennett was also instrumental in getting Robert S. Kerr elected as governor in 1942. On the national level, Bennett helped Kerr to write the keynote address to the 1944 Democratic National Convention that Bennett attended as a state delegate. He later helped to get Kerr elected as state senator. The two would often consult and assist each other in their careers.

International Dreams

As Bennett expanded his contacts with fellow dreamers and his visits beyond Oklahoma, he also began to expand his dreams beyond the state's borders. It is not certain where Bennett began his contact with and interest in internationals and minorities. It is very likely that as a young boy in Arkadelphia, Arkansas, he had met international students at Ouachita College. There were children of missionaries who attended the college. Bennett would have encountered minority groups in his book sales across Oklahoma and Kansas. In the public schools in Oklahoma, Bennett would have dealt with native-American students and families. Henry and Vera Bennett kept an interest in providing an education to minorities within and without Oklahoma. Vera was educated in a Presbyterian Indian school in Durant and spoke Choctaw. Henry attended a national conference on educating Negroes in the late 1940s. Both were involved in the lives of international students on campus as well as with alumni.

Bennett's leadership and reputation at Oklahoma A & M, plus the growing recognition by the United States Agricultural Department, offered high recommendations for his assistance with international problems following World War II. The United Nations had been chartered in 1945. One of its first priorities was to deal with the problem of the war's destruction of food production abilities. Secretary of Agriculture, Clinton P. Anderson, appointed Henry as one of twenty-four delegates (the only American agricultural college president) to the Quebec International Food and Agricultural Organization. The meetings began in November, 1945. Bennett recorded his thoughts and impressions in articles sent to the *Stillwater News Press*. In the articles, Bennett described the problems and challenges facing the countries of Europe. He also described his suggestions and dreams for answering the challenges. He summed up his thoughts with the statement that "technical assistance from some of the highly developed countries will be sent to these undeveloped countries." This was the clear message of the Point Four program that Henry would later direct. At the conference Bennett met with A & M international alumni who had returned home and worked in high, governmental positions.

Four years later, Bennett's services would again be requested by the federal government. In early 1949 Richard C. O'Brien, chief of the overseas branch of the department of Army in Washington, D. C., officially invited Bennett to go on an eight-week assignment to the German "Trizonia"—the western divide of Germany controlled by the U.S./British/French occupation following World War II. His task was to assemble a survey suggesting development and progressive measures that would stabilize agricultural production. On August 24, 1949, Bennett sent his final report to the United States High Commissioner, John J. McCloy. In that report Henry made observations, conclusions and recommendations. He added follow-up reports and personal meetings with Mr. McCloy to complete his task. Many of his implemented recommendations were followed by dramatic improvements in agricultural production. Bennett had covered over 25,000 miles in completing his assignment.

Within a year, Bennett was once again requested for international assistance, meeting with another fellow dreamer. In early 1950, Ethiopian Emperor Haile Selassie invited Bennett "to visit the North African country of Abyssinia as advisor to Ethiopian educators and agriculturalists on the organization of an agricultural training center along the lines of land-grant colleges." On his return to the United States, Bennett stopped in Washington, D. C. to visit his old friend and political ally, Senator Robert Kerr. As was his custom after foreign travels, Bennett kept Kerr apprised of his findings and observations. Kerr realized the significance of Bennett's most recent insights and arranged for Bennett to visit with President Truman about the Ethiopian experiences and future possibilities. They shared their mutual beliefs of the need for educational aid to these underdeveloped, war-torn countries. After their brief meeting, Truman requested Kerr "to ask Bennett to write me a report of his trip to Ethiopia. I was very much impressed in what he had to say... and I would like to have a record of his conversation so I can give it more study." As a result of this trip, the Emperor accepted Bennett's recommendation to establish an agricultural college. Bennett was appointed to oversee the project. He would not only give good construction advice, but also make Oklahoma A & M faculty and staff available to assist in the college's development. As a lasting result the Alemaya University in Ethiopia continues to be in operation today.

The most dramatic convergence of fellow dreamers came with the creation of the Point Four program. The key dreamers were all involved: President Harry S. Truman, William Holloway, Benjamin Hardy, Robert S. Kerr, James E. Webb, Emperor Haile Selassie and Henry Garland Bennett. There was also a dramatic convergence of the idea, approval, leadership and organization for such a program. The very concept and announcement of the Point Four program were challenging. President Truman presented the concept of the Point Four program as a surprise addition to his State of the Union address on January 20, 1949. Truman presented three approved courses of action for peace and freedom following World War II. First, was total support for the United Nations and related agencies; second, was a continuation of current programs for world economic recovery; and third, was the strengthening of freedom-loving nations against the dangers of aggression. Secretly included was a "fourth point" that follows:

> Fourth, we must embark on a bold new program for making the benefits of our scientific advances and industrial progress available for the improvement and growth of underdeveloped areas.
>
> For the first time in history, humanity possesses the knowledge and the skill to relieve the suffering of these people. The United States is pre-eminent among the nations in the development of industrial and scientific techniques. The material resources which we can

afford to use for assistance of other people are limited. But our imponderable resources in technical knowledge are constantly growing and are inexhaustible.

I believe that we should make available to peace-loving peoples the benefit of our store of technical knowledge in order to help them realize their aspirations for a better life. And, in cooperation with other nations, we should foster capital investment in areas needing development.

Our aim should be to help the free peoples of the world, through their own efforts, to produce more food, more clothing, more materials for housing, and more mechanical power to lighten their burdens.

The process leading up to those words was an exercise in clandestine activities and the persistence of fellow dreamer, Benjamin Hardy. The implementation of those ideas were to be hard-fought, internal governmental battles. In the preceding fall, President Truman had just won a miraculous national election. The State Department was experiencing infighting over programs for foreign aid. Before the election a post-Truman mentality was creating battles for power and agency control. Yet within the State Department a lower-level, public relations expert, Benjamin Hardy, would produce the seeds of the Point Four concept. Because his superiors strongly opposed his ideas, they were secretly communicated through White House channels to President Truman. Hardy's ideas seemed to perfectly match the kind of program that President Truman wanted but was unable to get developed through the State Department leadership. It took many months before Congress gave its approval and temporary funding. The program needed a wise and knowledgeable leader who was not caught up in the State Department politics. Henry Garland Bennett was selected by the president in November, 1950. His selection was influenced by his past work in international programs, his long friendships within the Department of Agriculture, and personal lobbying by Bennett supporters including former Governor William Holloway, Senator Robert Kerr and Undersecretary of State James Webb.

Bennett was given a leave of absence from his duties at Oklahoma A & M. He began to develop his organization by employing Benjamin Hardy as his assistant. He fought to keep the program from being swallowed up by other threatened State Department agencies. He fought to get the proper funding from Congress. Bennett's appointment, since he was a State Department outsider, was another hurdle in getting the program organized and operating. There was infighting between the Institute of Inter-American Affairs (IIAA), the Marshall plan staff and the United States Department of Agriculture (USDA). The IIAA was active in South America with the Servico program. The USDA was upset over infringement in the agricultural area. The Marshall plan (Economic Cooperation Administration) had already put Point Four, officially called the Technical Cooperation Agency (TCA) under its organizational chart. It was recalled that Bennett set up his office in a "ramshackle temporary building that stood next to the Interior Department and the Agriculture Department." This allowed meetings with and recruitment of friends and colleagues of the two departments.

The State Department's initial introduction of the Mutual Security Act to Congress "made a broad sweep of foreign aid, but did not even mention Point IV." Truman had decided to consolidate the military, Point Four and the Marshall Plan under Averil Harriman, as head of the Mutual Security Administration—combining three agencies. But the Point Four concept was still not accepted by the traditional State Department hierarchy, because department leaders felt access and control of funding for their programs was threatened. Dr. Bennett approached his new colleague, Stanley Andrews, who was loaned to Bennett from the Department of Agriculture. Andrews and Bennett had been working together for twenty years. He told Andrews, "My God, Stanley, we're out. Without a title designating the Technical Cooperation Administration (Point Four) as a part of this bill, we haven't got anything; we're gone and the Marshall plan takes over. The boys made a pretty shrewd move there on the bill." He saw the importance of having the titled program in that bill. Andrews was in agreement and offered to get a title and take it directly to Senator Fulbright, Senate Appropriations Committee member, with an explanation. Andrews and Bennett went to their new office and consulted with the new staff about a title name for the program. After some discussion, Delia Kuhn, who was the public affairs worker in Dr. Bennett's office said, "Let's call it Point IV because this is Mr. Truman's deal.'"

Andrews gave an account of his meeting with Senator Fulbright:

> We fixed up a title to be inserted in the bill and I went over to Senator Fulbright and told him the same. 'I don't know if you know it or not, but this bill that's before your committee doesn't even have Dr. Bennett's organization or program in it at all. It's completely out.'

He said, 'I didn't know that.' He asked that we fix up a title to be inserted. I took a piece of paper out of my pocket, and handed it to him. He put it in his pocket, and went over to the Foreign Relations Committee and inserted this new language, and Point IV was born. That's just how close we came to getting left out.

Andrews, in oral interviews, commented about Henry Bennett and the Point Four program:

Dr. Bennett was a very simple fellow and a very plain guy. He could handle Congress and he could handle almost anybody. He was to some extent scared of this deal because there was pressure all the time for more and more money. Some of the State Department people wanted to pour in a lot of money as did the Marshall Plan people.

With the infighting and organization still in dispute, Stanley Andrews remembered how it all got resolved. They went to the president and asked for guidance. Truman then directed "the State Department to call in representatives of other relevant agencies, Agriculture, Public Health, Interior, Commerce and bureaus in Commerce to work out a program." Since no program was able to be created to mutual satisfaction, Truman called in all parties to the White House cabinet room for a meeting. Andrews then recounted the following events of the meeting:

State Department, Marshall plan and others had their say on what kind of a program we should undertake in this new venture. Dr. Bennett made his presentation last. Armed with a sheaf of telegrams and letters from church organizations, country bankers, educational groups and farm organizations, he turned to the globe which Mr. Truman always had around his office and the Cabinet Room and briefly sketched out what he thought were the greatest needs of the new nations at that time emerging in the world as the outcome of World War II. He had been to Ethiopia in the summer before he was appointed administrator and looked over the marvelous natural resources of that African nation, steeped in poverty, disease and hunger. He argued quite persuasively what a down-to-earth program might do to lift the living standards of the people of that country with the assertions that about two-thirds of the population of the world were living in the same conditions and that they had to be given some hope if free government were to survive. He coined a rather telling phrase which stuck around for quite awhile. 'These people,' he said, 'must have a chance to at least glance into the door of the Twentieth

Century.' Mr. Truman turned to the group and said simply, 'That's the kind of a program I was talking about.' So that was that and we went away and began to build on that principle.

With the president's decision expressed, Bennett was more secure in his authority and direction, and there was the need to enlist able assistants and secure congressional financial support. Ben Hardy was on board and would be a committed colleague. There was mutual respect between them. Bennett was able to enlist the help and support of Raymond W. Miller, Stanley Andrews, and Merwin L. Bihan. Stanley Andrews recalled that:

> The organization that was finally put together was made up of castoffs from other bureaus. Dr. Bennett was about the only new guy in it. The rest of them were from the Interior Department, Agricultural Department, the Treasury, The Budget Bureau and Public Health. In some cases the Department dumped their surplus over to us. I was still in the Department of Agriculture, where a portion of the Latin American program was administered. We finally got a little organization; I think it had less than 300 people set up.

Just as the State Department, Congress was certainly not prepared for Henry Bennett. He was later described as "one of those old fashioned Americans who didn't believe in wasting public money… he consistently urged Congress to give him less money than it was prepared to appropriate." Reporters told of how many "cabinet officers and generals would testify before Congressional committees on the mutual security aid bill, of which Doctor Bennett's program was a fractional part, and most of them came away with flushed faces and reddened ears from the quizzing of lawmakers." Bennett, in homely, earthly language outlined his program of self-help as "the cheapest form of foreign aid…" In June of 1951, Dr. Bennett, appearing before the Senate Foreign Relations Committee, summed up the long term aim of Point Four: "We work ourselves out of business… as soon as possible the nationals of the country take leadership." This was very contrary to other national foreign assistance programs that only wanted to grow in size and power.

Bennett took a hands-on approach with Point Four just as he had as a college president. He traveled extensively and met face to face with international leaders. Where invited, he evaluated the immediate needs in that country and made recommendations for technical assistance and the country's involvement. He was able to involve many Oklahoma A & M friends to assist in the work. He traveled through Central and South America, made a second trip to Ethiopia, a second trip to Europe and was planning on trips to the Near East and the Far East. His wife, Vera, accompanied him on several of these trips. He made regular reports to the State Department and to President Truman. He traveled throughout the United States giving speeches to inform the nation of the program, its intents and its progress. In January, 1951, a *Time* magazine article entitled "Plows and Sacred Cows," summarized the effectiveness of the Point Four philosophy and activities. Bennett reported that "a former county agent from North Carolina named Horace Holmes went to India as an adviser on village improvement to the Indian government. He was sent to a bedraggled northern section of the country, where he concentrated on 100 square miles near Mahwa in the United Provinces." A majority of the population were illiterate, starving and infested with disease and parasites. The land was also populated with the sacred cows of India who roamed free and competed for the meager crops available. Holmes never challenged the place of scared cows in the Indian culture. He "let them alone, but he eventually tricked them without sacrilege by introducing legume crops that they would not eat." The article then described the educational tactics that were at the core of the Point Four program:

> Carefully avoiding taboos and deeply rooted customs, Holmes succeeded in getting farmers to plant a new kind of Indian wheat (Punjab 591). In the first season it yielded 43% more than the old-style wheat. Next year Punjab 591 was planted by entire villages, and even spread outside the experimental area. The increase went up to 63% when Homes showed the farmers how to rotate their wheat crop with soil-improving legumes. With potatoes Holmes had the same success. A new variety increased the yield by 112%.

> After Holmes had won the farmers' confidence, he took the next step: teaching them how to use improved, but still simple tools, e.g., turning plows and five-tooth cultivators. A simple form of thresher introduced by Holmes made it possible for his farmers to thresh their wheat crop in three days instead of ten. The seven days saved allowed many farmers to plow their land for the next crop before the soil under the wheat stubble got too hard.

In addition to life-saving improvements, Holmes was also able to introduce the use and effectiveness of fertilizer, insecticides and cattle immunization. He set up village schools to continually educate the villagers as to modern agricultural techniques. By July, 1951, Bennett was directing 139 projects in 34 countries. Under his supervision were 397 Point Four technicians. It was reported that "by offering technical aid and scientific aid to those who requested it, Point Four helped to reduce famine, disease, and the economic hardships of 35 African and Asian nations by 1953." Point Four also became the "godfather to a host of American foreign assistance programs, including the Peace Corps, which followed in the next decades." One of Bennett's finest speeches explaining the Point Four concept was given to the American Vocational Association Convention in Minneapolis, Minnesota, on November 28, 1951. Hardy certainly had a part of the speech preparation. In the speech Bennett stated:

> Food, health and education: these three essentials have consumed the bulk of our energies and our funds in the first year of the Program. Not only are they the keys to eventual economic and social progress, but they are the things that the people of the underdeveloped areas themselves most ardently and earnestly desire. I have said that Point 4 cooperation is designed to help people do what they want to do. That is not a pious statement of policy. It is a practical rule for getting good and quick, concrete results.

Tragic Death and Legacy

The dreams were being made real and the fellow dreamers were gratified with the progress. In late 1951 Henry and Vera Bennett, Benjamin Hardy and other top aids began an ambitious long trip to recruit, observe and evaluate the Point Four operations. They planned to go to Rome, Italy; Athens, Greece; Cairo, Egypt; Amman, Jordan; Beirut, Lebanon; Damascus, Syria; Baghdad, Iraq; Teheran Iran; Karachi, Pakistan; Dehli, Bombay, Colombo, Madras, and Calcutta, India; Ceylon; Bangkok, Thailand; Hong Kong; and Tokyo, Japan. Their scheduled return was set for January 27, 1952. The first stop in Rome was to give an address to the Sixth Session of the United Nations Food and Agricultural Organization (FAO) on December 4, 1951. Bennett had been an official representative to the first meeting of the organization in Quebec in 1945. It is very likely that Hardy helped with preparing the address. In his speech Bennett said:

All of us together can be proud of the accomplishments of FAO, but proud as we are of the achievements up to date, all of us I know must realize that we are losing the fight of increasing food production as compared with increasing population in the world. We have had the report from the Director-General that while the population of the world has grown 12% since World War II, we have increased food production only 9%, so we must face reality that we are losing the fight and it is not necessary. We can win the fight. It can be won because we have enough scientific and technical knowledge available, if applied, to produce sufficient food to feed adequately and well all of the teeming millions of the world.

By mid-December, 1951, the team was already days behind schedule. They were tired but excited by the progress of their visits. One of the biggest challenges was their next stop—Iran. The contentious government had not yet agreed to the required declaration for receiving funds with the deadline only two weeks away. The team had scheduled a five-day visit and with threatening weather, they wanted no other trip delays. They left the Baghdad airport on the evening of December 22 and headed northeast for Teheran. The Egyptian Airlines plane had sixteen passengers including Henry and Vera Bennett, Benjamin Hardy, James T. Mitchell and A. Cyril Crilley. The plane encountered a blinding snowstorm just outside of Teheran. The Mehrabad airport was located very high at 4,000 feet alongside of the lofty Elburz range to the north and other smaller mountain ranges to the south and east. The airport kept in radio contact, sending up repeated flares to light the runway. The circling plane reported a little after 8:00 p.m. that the runway had been sighted. They attempted to land several times but were unsuccessful. The United States Ambassador, Loy Henderson, and his staff heard the plane propellers but were unable to see the plane because of the weather and darkness. There was no further contact from the plane. They assumed that the pilot had given up trying to land at an unfamiliar airport and returned to Baghdad. After confirming that the plane had not returned to Baghdad, a search party set out at 6:00 a.m. the next morning. They found the scattered trail of wreckage, about 300 yards long, two and a half miles north of the airport in what was called the "red or danger area, which pilots are supposed to avoid when coming in for a landing." The wheels were down indicating plans for another attempted landing. All on board were killed. In the scattered wreckage the bodies were badly burned making identification difficult. But Henry and Vera Bennett's bodies had both been thrown clear of the wreckage. They were found near each other and among their nearby belongings was an open, family Bible. The bodies of the Point Four team were flown back to the United States. It was ironic that the very first official contract agreement was between Point Four and Iran and that the last efforts of Henry Bennett, Benjamin Hardy and the Point Four team were in Iran seeking to complete the details of that agreement.

Responses from the national leaders were immediate. It was the day before Christmas and the grief was deeply felt. President Truman released the following statement:

> In the death of Henry Garland Bennett, administrator of the Point Four program, I have lost a friend and the American people have lost a great teacher of the simple ideas of cooperation and brotherhood.
>
> He was a good man, and he believed in the goodness of human nature; he was an educated man, in the best sense, and he believed in the right of all to an education. Finally, he understood how people could make miracles by sharing knowledge to help themselves and each other. That is the essence of the Point Four program, for which Dr. Bennett lived and died.

Then Secretary of State, Dean Acheson, issued the following statement:

> Dr. Bennett was one of those rare human beings whose faith in his fellowmen inspired them to unselfish action far beyond their duty and their ordinary capabilities.
>
> Dr. Bennett believed in the Point Four program, because he, in his long, rich life, had seen what people working together, could accomplish to help themselves and one another, against great odds. He believed in Point Four, and he gave to the program and the people working together in it the whole wealth of his knowledge, his enthusiasm and his faith.

Oklahoma Senator Robert Kerr indicated in his statement that Henry Bennett was "a dreamer of no little dreams with the magic of transporting them into reality." Assistant Secretary of State, James

Webb included the following words in his statement:

> ...I am convinced that this [Point Four] growth was possible because Dr. Bennett was driven by a single passion—he loved his fellow men. This love was wise, understanding, and above all practical.

> ...But love alone could not have done what Dr. Bennett accomplished. In addition, he had great ability, driving energy, and the gift of leadership.

On Thursday, January 10, 1952, a memorial service was held in the Oklahoma A & M fieldhouse in Stillwater, Oklahoma. Some 7,500 persons, "from cowhands to the Secretary of Agriculture," gathered as one to honor the two lives. The next day burial services were held at the Highland Cemetery at Durant, Oklahoma. The graves were very simple and were next to Henry's father and mother, Thomas Jefferson and Mary Elizabeth Bright Bennett.

Walker Stone was the editor of the Scripps-Howard Newspaper Alliance and a personal friend of Henry Bennett. Upon hearing of Henry's death, he wrote a personal letter to the family accompanied by copies of an editorial he had written for his nationally syndicated newspapers. He described Henry Bennett as an "oddity in present-day Washington Officialdom," and "one of those old-fashioned Americans who didn't believe in wasting public money." He gave a brief overview of Bennett's struggle to maintain the Point Four integrity:

> When he refused to allow the Point Four program to become a gravy train, the bureaucrats tried to take it away from him so that it could be blown up into a bigger and a permanent 'Marshall Plan' which would keep them on the payroll. But Congress decided in favor of Dr. Bennett.

Stone included in his editorial an example of Bennett's encounter with the Congressional Appropriations Committee:

> When Congress was asked to appropriate money to buy $4500 combines for peasants in Iran, Dr. Bennett was asked to comment because he was familiar with Iran. 'They wouldn't know what to do with a combine,' he said. But he added, 'it would be helpful to buy some iron points to put on their wooden plows. They would cost

about 75 cents apiece.' Congress recently voted Dr. Bennett $200,000,000 more than he requested, by transferring to his control some projects which had been initiated by the Economic Co-Operation Administration. After looking over the projects, Dr. Bennett told a friend that he thought he would save the money and turn it back to the taxpayers.

Stone concluded his editorial with a personal tribute to Bennett: "He was a great man, deeply devoted to high principles and humble virtues which made his country great. He will be mourned by thousands whom he befriended during a long and useful lifetime."

In President Truman's last State of the Union speech in January, 1952, he mentioned the following:

> We have recently lost a great public servant who was leading this effort to bring opportunity and hope to the people of half the world. Dr. Bennett and his associates died in the line of duty on a Point 4 mission. It is up to us to carry on the great work for which they gave their lives.

The impact of Bennett's life and dreams remained with former President Truman for many years. On January 18, 1956, he wrote in a letter to Mrs. Eleanor Roosevelt

> Dr. Bennett of Oklahoma A & M, who worked with me on the Point IV program, spent the previous year in Ethiopia where he found a plateau of about 62,000 square miles at from six to eight thousand feet above sea level where the soil is as rich and black as it is in the Iowa corn belt. His estimate was that it could raise enough food for a hundred million people.

With the new rounds of State Department infighting and the new Eisenhower administration coming into office, Point Four was absorbed into other State Department agencies staffed with part-time leadership. It eventually disappeared in the mid 1950s giving rise to the "ugly American" concept of foreign aid. Not until ten years later would the program concept be renewed in the Peace Corps, for which it was considered in its creation to be named after Henry Bennett. The State Department today carries on a program entitled United States Agency for International Development (USAID) that has the intention of continuing the Point Four philosophy.

Although the story of Henry Bennett has been suppressed by the passing of time, it has been rediscovered by a new generation hungry for positive role models and good American foreign relations. Numerous lasting memorials are present to remind us of the Bennett legacy. The Alemaya University founded in 1954 in Ethiopia is a continuing monument to the ideals and dreams of Henry Bennett and Emperor Haile Selassie. Oklahoma State University in Stillwater built a contemporary Bennett Memorial Chapel on campus in 1957 with former Governor William J. Holloway as guest speaker. OSU's School of International Studies also established the Henry G. Bennett Distinguished Service Award in 1969. Southeast Oklahoma State University in Durant dedicated the Henry G. Bennett Memorial Library in 1982 with William J. Holloway, Jr. as the guest speaker. In 1990 the Oklahoma A & M class of 1940 dedicated a ten-foot statue of Henry Bennett located on campus which overlooks the physical accomplishments of his "twenty-five year plan." In 1997 OSU established the International Education and Outreach Program (OSUIEO) housed in the present Wes Watkins Center. This beautiful facility houses numerous programs that continue the dreams and programs of Henry Bennett. In the center is a room dedicated to Point Four with an emphasis on the relationship between Oklahoma A & M and Ethiopia. In April, 2007, a permanent display was dedicated to Henry Bennett in the Oklahoma History Center in Oklahoma City. The local Bennett family members were present to dedicate this display which is the only one in the history center devoted to the memory of a single individual. Bennett's impact on many aspects of Oklahoma education, growth and history warranted this honor.

Henry and Vera Bennett left an amazing legacy of education and facilitation of self help. Many Oklahoma college graduates can point to the Bennett's lives as being instrumental in their completion of a college education. Many future leaders around the world would point to the Bennetts as models and co-laborers in the struggle to help humankind meet the basic needs of all people. Besides brick and mortar reminders, another important legacy was left in the lives of the Bennett children, grandchildren and great-grandchildren that continues even today. Many of these have expanded on Bennett's dreams of helping others to improve their lives. May they be blessed through uniting with other "fellow dreamers" in accomplishing great things for all humankind.

Chapter Two

William Judson Holloway

A lifelong friend and supporter of the dreams

One of the longest personal friendships of Henry Garland Bennett was with William Judson Holloway. They were fellow dreamers who provided mutual support and respect throughout their lives. They grew up in the same neighborhood and shared a common religious faith. Although both were from poor families, they shared interests and a thirst for education. This pattern for lifelong learning enhanced both their personal and professional lives. Both were ambitious young men who encouraged each other's success. Their sons continue a friendship to the present day.

Background of a Dreamer

William Holloway was born December 15, 1888 in Arkadelphia, Arkansas, to Stephen Lee and Molly Horne Holloway. William's father was a successful minister in Baptist churches in Arkansas, Oklahoma and Texas. His father had been educated and trained at Ouachita College in Arkadelphia, graduating in 1896. William's mother died when he was four years old in 1892. That was about the same time that Henry Bennett, then six years old, and his family moved to Arkadelphia and built their boarding house.

Young Henry began a friendship with the younger William and took him by the hand to the Ouachita primary school. As children of ministers, they were both able to attend the school at no cost. It was likely that William's father traveled in his ministry services just as Henry's father did. William eventually became a boarder in the Bennett boarding house. Throughout their college experiences Henry and William competed for forensic honors in speech and debate through their campus literary societies. Both were active in other campus activities with a third close friend, Coulter Hamilton Moses. They were called the "Three Arkansas Musketeers." Usually one of the three won top honors in the campus events. Each was glad when the other graduated, thereby improving their chances of winning top campus honors.

Holloway graduated from Ouachita with a bachelor of arts degree in 1910. He began attending classes at the University of Chicago that summer. He had been promised a public school teaching job in the fall. The job fell through and Holloway was left with no direction. It is not certain who contacted the other first, but Bennett did offer Holloway a teaching job in Hugo, Oklahoma, where Bennett was superintendent. Holloway accepted the offer with advance money from Bennett to travel to Hugo.

Preparing for the Dreams

In the fall of 1910 Holloway became the elementary school principal at Hugo. When Henry Bennett was promoted to county superintendent, he promoted Holloway to be principal of the Hugo high school. In recruiting new teachers for the district, Bennett followed the habit of looking back to Ouachita College in Arkadelphia, Arkansas. He and Holloway were looking through the recent graduation photos to contact possible recruits. Holloway noticed a particularly attractive young lady from Texarkana, Arkansas, Amy Arnold, whom he had never met. They contacted her and she accepted the teaching position in Hugo.

While working as principal, Holloway began pursuing his interest in law by studying at night. He took a leave of absence in the fall of 1914, having been admitted to the law school of Cumberland University in Lebanon, Tennessee. He returned to Hugo a year later with his law degree in hand. He gained admittance to the Oklahoma state bar and started a private practice in Hugo.

Holloway found that a law degree in Hugo, Oklahoma was not the key to financial success. Wishing to add to his income, he ran for prosecuting attorney of Choctaw County. He won the election in 1916. With his professional dreams being realized and his personal income more secure, Holloway began to develop interest in other areas of his life.

At an evening social event in Hugo he met a young lady, Amy Arnold. Amy was a recent graduate of Ouachita College in Arkadelphia.

She had been recruited, with others, by Henry Bennett to come to Hugo and teach. On June 16, 1917, they were married in Texarkana, Arkansas, where her parents lived and worked. Amy was the daughter of Richard W. and Fanny Knuckles Arnold. They had moved from Paducah, Kentucky.

The newly-married couple returned to Hugo and established a home. Their dreams were detoured with the outbreak of World War I. Holloway volunteered for officer's school and was sent for training during October and November, 1918, to Camp Zachary Taylor near Louisville, Kentucky. The war ended before Holloway could be sent overseas. A 1920 federal census listed "W. J. Holloway, husband, age 31 and Amy A., wife, age 25." as residents of Choctaw County, Oklahoma.

Holloway expanded his ambitions by entering the state senatorial campaign in 1920 for the twenty-fourth district of Choctaw, McCurtain and Pushmataha counties. He won the election and became active in state politics. As a state senator, Holloway gained a reputation as "an affable and energetic legislator." He was elected by his peers to serve as president pro tempore of the Oklahoma state senate. Holloway was popular with his local supporters. He championed educational causes and supported actions that benefited teachers and schools. These same causes and actions were strongly supported by Bennett. Holloway worked hard at maintaining good relationships with his constituents. He kept up correspondence and the usual political favors for his close friends and supporters. He provided railroad passes for his lifelong friend, Henry Bennett, and others. His began a second term in 1924 when he ran without opposition.

The political situation in Oklahoma state government at that time was volatile. With a governor being impeached and Holloway serving, at times, as acting governor; it was assumed by many that he would run for governor in 1926. Instead, he sought the position of lieutenant governor. With strong support and assistance from his family and friends, Holloway won the election against twelve other candidates. He actually carried every county in Oklahoma. He took office in January, 1927, along with Governor Henry S. Johnston.

Almost immediately, Governor Johnson's term was one of controversy and widespread disunity. He was accused of incompetency and delayed a call for impeachment by asking the Oklahoma National Guard not to allow the legislature to meet in what was deemed "an illegal assembly." During this time, Holloway worked to maintain neutrality in the party disputes and infighting. He was also active in working with his friend, Harry B. Cordell, president of the Oklahoma Board of Agriculture, to secure a new president for Oklahoma A & M College in Stillwater. Holloway worked to get his friend Henry Bennett nominated as the new president. Bennett had been president of the Southeastern State Teacher's College in Durant for nine years. Bennett's growing reputation combined with Holloway's strong endorsement was enough to overcome the past charges of political cronyism in that important position. In the past such educational positions were filled on the basis of political allegiance instead of competency and friendship. Henry Bennett was elected and became the president of Oklahoma A & M College in 1928. He would remain president there for twenty-three years.

Governorship of Oklahoma: Keeping the Dream from Becoming a Nightmare

The resentment of Governor Johnson continued to escalate. Finally in early 1929, the state senate approved articles of impeachment against the governor. William Holloway assumed the position of acting governor during the impeachment trial. It was a difficult time for Holloway. He continued to work hard to maintain neutrality in all of his leadership efforts. He deferred many major state issues until the impeachment issue was settled. These actions along with his previous good reputation in senate activities promoted confidence in him from all party factions. Following the impeachment trial, Johnson was removed from office and William Judson Holloway became Oklahoma's eighth governor on March 20, 1929.

While the promotion of Holloway to governor was a great personal honor, the position of governor in Oklahoma was held in little esteem. There was much criticism within and without the state regarding the position. Holloway would bring his strong ethical background, his love for positive leadership and his history of political reconciliation to this maligned position. He told the Oklahoma City Gibbons Club "My sole ambition is to serve honorably and efficiently; my hope is that at the end of the two years I still will have my self-respect." William and

Amy both maintained their lifestyle as "down to earth" people who were just "one of the people" instead of above the people. Such an attitude would also help him in national and international opportunities ahead.

Holloway began his administration with all efforts to be open and aboveboard. The state legislature had spent nearly all of its time in the impeachment battles. Little had been done to develop the legislative agendas for the state's welfare. Holloway had not had time to prepare a positive legislative agenda for consideration. With thoughtful attention in consideration of the state's best interests, Holloway asked the legislature to adjourn until he was prepared for them to meet and consider the state's needs. The legislature agreed and time was allowed for partisanship and the state's negative image to cool off.

In establishing his administration's new state appointees, Holloway broke with longstanding political patronage, showing further evidence against a charge of cronyism. He told his fellow politicians "You may help make appointments for jobs at the capitol, but these appointees will get their walking papers unless they were thoroughly capable of holding their jobs." Low salaries made the challenge of enlisting qualified and capable state workers very difficult.

Holloway's first legislative program reduced the controversial and powerful state highway commission from five members to three. When selecting the chairman of the Oklahoma Highway Commission, Holloway shook past traditions by offering the position to a Republican millionaire. Although some in both parties were wary of the political future of such a powerful position, all agreed that the wealthy man would certainly be above charges of corruption. In April, 1929, Louis (Lew) Haynes Wentz of Ponca City, accepted the position. Two Democrats accepted the other highway commission positions creating effective leadership in meeting the state's major need.

The state of Oklahoma was only twenty-two years old. The challenges were great in many areas. The most immediate concern was the state's poor highway system. Three-fourths of the state's 6,289 miles of highways were unpaved while the number of motor vehicles in the state had doubled from 1924 to 1929. Another concern was the state's financial picture. The legislature had adjourned before approving an appropriations bill. The state had accumulated a significant debt from the previous year, causing the conscientious Holloway to reluctantly veto a large school aid bill. To many this illustrated Holloway's concern for setting the right priorities. The new governor worked with key state senators to prepare a proposed budget that met state needs and eliminated the state's debt. Holloway was intent on restoring confidence and respectability in a state government that was viewed as contentious and without principle.

On May 16, 1929, Holloway convened the special legislative session. As the state senators and representatives gathered at the joint meeting to hear the governor's proposals, Holloway began his speech on a note of financial responsibility. He told the group that his office did not have sufficient funds to make copies of his speech and encouraged them to take notes. He strongly encouraged financial responsibility with the proposed budget. He also threatened to veto any excessive appropriations sent to him. The rest of his speech involved reforms for the state departments and institutions. In addressing the needs of higher education in the state, Holloway stated:

> There is no excuse for a spirit of competition developing among the higher institutions of learning in the State of Oklahoma. The only thing we want to consider is the welfare of all the people in this state; that is all! We are not trying to build up anything for any individual nor any town in this state, but we have the problem of unifying the policy for higher education in this state.

This may have been directed at those who were concerned with Henry Bennett's first year as president of Oklahoma A & M and Holloway's personal friendship and influence. He also expressed his concern over the governor's involvement on the state's textbook commission. He stated in his up-front manner:

> Now, I used to teach school from 1910 to 1914, and from 1914 up to this good hour I haven't seen the inside of a textbook. Now, what in the world would I know about adopting textbooks, and what I say about myself applies to every Governor that ever sat in the Governor's office in Oklahoma.

> Now, what good excuse is there to leave the Governor upon this Commission? Why should it not be best for the children of this state and for the people to permit an intelligent, efficient expert to be appointed on that board?

Therefore, I sincerely want you, in tackling this problem, to reconstitute that commission and leave the Governor off of it.

The twelfth legislative session adjourned on July 5, 1929. Holloway was able, through mandates and legislative actions, to implement several significant programs for the state. A statewide speed limit of 45 miles per hour was set to increase public safety. He was able to get a resolution passed to create toll bridges along an established western state border. Some Oklahoma schools were overseen by as many as three separate boards creating confusion and animosity. Holloway was able to get a bill approved creating a coordinating board of various college administrators. He was also able to establish a permanent textbook commission for approving textbooks in the state. The confusing, local teacher certification, which had differing county standards, was eliminated in favor of a centralized, state standard through the Oklahoma Board of Education. He was also able to provide direct state funding for "weak schools" in the state as well as increase salaries for some state officials. He brought reform to the state's election laws. A primary runoff system was created requiring a candidate to hold a clear majority to obtain the party nomination. Holloway signed a bill allowing funding for the construction of a building to house the Oklahoma Historical Society.

Some issues presented by Holloway failed to be enacted. After the session adjourned, there were the customary, mutual charges of bribery and drunkenness among legislators creating negative rumors again throughout the state. There was also concern that Holloway would follow the path of past governors and try to implement the failed actions of the legislature through questionable executive mandates. Again Holloway sought to provide assurance and confidence in his role as governor. He said "There has been a feeling that when the legislature adjourned and you members are back home, hell will break loose and this department will go helter-skelter. It will not make any difference in my conduct whether you are in session or not."

One major event that threatened the economic stability of the state as well as the entire nation was the Wall Street crash of October 29, 1929. The country, as well as Oklahoma, was entering the challenges of the Great Depression. All of Holloway's plans for economic stability with the state budget were set aside. He was forced to spend well above the state's revenues to keep the state from a total collapse of services. The downward drop of petroleum prices affected the state significantly. Unemployment in the state rose dramatically causing scenes of bread lines in Oklahoma City. In January, 1930, the state experienced one of the worst blizzards in history.

In an attempt to meet the many state needs, Holloway was able to persuade several prominent state leaders to serve on special commissions in order to address some of the depression-related challenges. Grants were obtained from the federal government to help purchase seeds for the state's farmers. State banks were given encouragement to liquidate or consolidate. The state highway department funds were used to employ state citizens in planned projects. Schools were given assistance with ideas for creative funding.

While Holloway maintained his reputation for state leadership which was above reproach, other state leaders in his administration corrupted politics with accusations and personal power plays. He was able to defend himself against a blatantly partisan lawsuit. Holloway was still able to display dignity in his office by demonstrating wise reactions and skillful dealings with offenders.

Holloway, as governor, was invited to be the speaker for commencement exercises at his alma mater, Ouachita College. He and his family made the trip back to Arkadelphia, Arkansas. As he spoke at commencement, his son William, Jr., then about seven years old, decided to explore the campus. He played around the campus fountain and fell in, ruining his new suit. His parents were informed and due punishment was administered.

Holloway's political star was rising in the state in spite of the partisan attacks. His character, integrity, and concern for the public led many to favor him as a leading candidate for the state's United States Senate race. He was certainly tempted to consider the possibility, but he stunned the state's political world with his announcement at a Sunday press conference on January 30, 1930. He declined the possibility of pursuing the Democratic party's nomination by stating that "I am profoundly grateful for the high honors already conferred upon me by my fellow citizens. I am happy to submerge my personal ambitions and fortunes, and do that which seems best for the welfare of my state and my party." The fact was that Holloway had decided not to run for any political office again.

Several factors certainly influenced his decision not to pursue another public office. The infighting and personal attacks were painful to endure. The prospects of his candidacy would cause further divisions within his party. The emotional and physical pressure of dealing with the Great Depression crises were enormous. But in reality, the most important reasons were his personal finances and family responsibilities. The office of governor paid very little but necessitated great personal expenses. Holloway needed to provide a more substantial income for his family. He could not do that ethically through politics alone. He had decided to go back to his law practice. He stated later in his life that "Public life is fine for people who can financially afford it, but there comes a time for people with average means to get back to their chosen work and accomplish something there." The state supreme court also ruled later that constitutionally Holloway could not succeed himself as governor even though he had not run as governor.

January 12, 1931 saw the completion of Holloway's term as governor. While some partisans in the state made their usual criticisms and baseless charges, others who were more credible gave a positive evaluation of his term. The *Tulsa World* noted in an editorial that "His personality and poise have been valuable and gratifying. The Holloway regime was conducted with responsibility and decorum." Holloway was recognized for his ability to step into the governor's office at a crucial time and bring stability to the state. The political turmoil was lessened by his actions and character. The enormous challenges of the Great Depression called for leadership with human concern and wise actions. Holloway's background, moral integrity and training gave him the resources to be such a leader.

Supporter of Dreams

Holloway remained in Oklahoma City and established his own home. He reestablished a very successful law practice with his half-brother Stephen D. Holloway. Although he never again ran for political office, he did agree to serve the state when asked. He was Oklahoma's first representative to the Interstate Oil Compact Commission in 1935 continuing for several decades. He actively campaigned and gave counsel for state and national Democratic candidates, especially Robert S. Kerr and John F. Kennedy. He also was active in fundraising for religious and civic organizations. Holloway was especially honored in 1968 when his son, William Holloway, Jr., was appointed by President Johnson to the United States Court of Appeals for the Tenth Circuit.

The state of Oklahoma was indeed fortunate to have a leader of such character and quality. It was also fortunate to have those same characteristics embraced by Holloway's son. William Holloway, Jr., was born in 1923 in Hugo, Oklahoma. He moved with his family to Oklahoma City in 1927. His college education at the University of Oklahoma was interrupted by his service in World War II. He received his bachelor of arts degree in 1947. He received his law degree from the Harvard Law School in 1950. He worked in his father's law firm in Oklahoma City, leaving to work in the Department of Justice in Washington, D. C., in 1951 and 1952. During his time in the nation's capitol, William, Jr. kept in contact with Henry and Vera Bennett. On the day that the Bennetts and the Point Four leaders left for their ill-fated trip, William, Jr. had invited the Bennetts to have breakfast with him at the top of the Hotel Washington. It seems only fitting that the last meal that the Bennetts would have in the United States would have been with the son of his lifelong friend. Upon hearing of their tragic deaths, William, Jr. went to express his sympathies to Tom Bennett, Henry and Vera's youngest son, who happened to be working in the Justice Department building at the same time.

Afterward, William, Jr. returned to Oklahoma City and worked in his father's law firm until his 1968 appointment as a U. S. Circuit Court Judge. He was able to serve as chief judge of the tenth circuit from September 1984 until September 1991. He had married Helen Hoehn of Enid, Oklahoma in 1963. They had two children: William Holloway III and Eleanor Gentry Holloway.

During his terms as lieutenant governor and governor, William Holloway maintained close personal contact with his friend Henry Bennett. Bennett was a frequent family visitor in the governor's mansion as well as in their Oklahoma City homes. Holloway was instrumental in getting Bennett elected to the new position as president of Oklahoma A & M College in Stillwater. But even during Bennett's time as president of the Durant school, Holloway was also helpful. Holloway used contacts to help get funding for new buildings on the campuses and increased operational funds. He was able to use his influence in the state and the nation to get Henry involved in federal funding and educational innovations on both campuses. It is also quite obvious that Henry Bennett used his considerable influence throughout the state to support Holloway in elections and legislative programs.

On December 15, 1964, William Holloway was encouraged by his family to attend a quiet 75th birthday dinner at the Sheraton-Oklahoma Hotel in Oklahoma City. He was met by over 800 guests there to honor him at a surprise William Holloway Appreciation dinner. The main address was given by his childhood and Ouachita College friend, C. Hamilton Moses, who was a lawyer and the former president of the Arkansas Power and Light Company. Hamilton called this meeting "a demonstration of friendship for the former governor" and recalled anecdotes of their life together in Arkansas and later in a fight against a federal power grab [electric power companies].

Among the other guests were those called to give "special exposures" on Holloway's life. These were Mrs. Homer Paul, Ned Looney, Senator Al Nichols, Jess Larson and Rev. Rupert Nanny. Two other speakers were of special connection to Holloway. One was Oklahoma Senator Robert S. Kerr. The other was Phil C. Bennett, the second son of his childhood friend, Henry Bennett. Holloway was presented a bound book of over 400 personal letters and was told of an additional 400 letters that would be bound for him in another volume.

During the celebration, President Lyndon Baines Johnson sent a personal telegram to be read to the guests in Holloway's presence. Johnson wrote of him:

> May I join with countless friends of Governor Holloway as they gather in tribute to him on Tuesday. Governor Holloway has earned the respect and admiration of Oklahomans and of Americans for his generous and forthright public service both as a public servant and as a private citizen. His wisdom and his fine character have added much to our national life and to the cause of good government. I hope that this is the first of many more birthday celebrations. With every good wish
>
> Lyndon B. Johnson.

William Holloway enjoyed six more years of life before his death on January 28, 1970, at the age of 81. His wife, Amy, died September 8, 1969. He was buried in Rose Hill Cemetery in Oklahoma City. His son William Holloway, Jr. is still, at 84, an active federal appellate court senior judge living and practicing in Oklahoma City. He maintains contact with his friend Tom Bennett who works in the same federal building.

Chapter Three

Robert S. Kerr

A political ally paving the way for the dreams

The first three dreamers had very similar backgrounds in their preparations for achieving their dreams. Bennett, Holloway and Kerr were born as commoners; each was from a devoutly Baptist home; each had to work hard when young; each was able to receive a good education; each developed a strong work ethic; each developed close personal working relationships; each was involved in Democratic politics; each was deeply committed to Oklahoma; and each had a strong sense of patriotism. They influenced each other in their personal and professional careers and all three would remain close, personal friends throughout their lives.

Background of a Dreamer

Robert Samuel Kerr also came from a family of dreamers. His parents, William Samuel Kerr and Margaret Eloda Wright Kerr left Milford, Texas with a packed, covered wagon and headed for the Indian Territory in 1894—thirteen years before Oklahoma would gain statehood. William was a farmer, a clerk and politician. The couple settled in Pontotoc County in the Chickasaw Nation. As many other new arrivals, the Kerrs leased 160 acres of timberland just southwest of the Ada community. They lived for a short while in a tent until a fourteen-foot-square log cabin was built. Robert Samuel Kerr was born there on September 11, 1896, allowing him to become the first, native-born governor in Oklahoma's history. He was the oldest son, the second of six children born to William and Margaret Kerr. The family moved closer to the town of Ada allowing Robert the chance to attend public schools. At the age of nine, Robert joined the local Baptist Church.

Early in his life Robert found the sound values of his father and mother were an important part of his own life. They were hard workers with the goal of family betterment in mind. They were honest folk who valued the importance of a dollar and a full day's work. His father was a strong Democrat, a Southern Baptist Sunday School teacher and a teetotaler. Robert worked hard as a youth. At the age of fifteen, he picked as much as 396 pounds of cotton per day.

Kerr entered East Central Oklahoma Normal School in Ada in the fall of 1909. He completed a two-year high school course. He entered the newly-opened Oklahoma Baptist University at Shawnee. The Baptist school was forced to close the next year and Kerr continued for another year at East Central. He completed the requirements for a certificate to teach. He taught in a country school for two years. In the fall of 1915, Kerr borrowed three hundred and fifty dollars and continued his education at the University of Oklahoma in Norman studying law. Because of financial hardships, Kerr was forced to quit the university after only one year. He accepted a job as a magazine salesman in Webb City, Missouri. A particularly impressive sales pitch was made to a local attorney, B. Robert Elliott. The lawyer told him, "I don't give a damn about your magazines, but I'll give you a salary of one hundred dollars a month to work for me." Kerr accepted on the provision that the lawyer purchase a magazine subscription. He worked there until the spring of 1917 when the United States entered World War I. Kerr reported to Fort Logan H. Root, near Little Rock, Arkansas. He was commissioned as a second lieutenant in artillery. His unit was assigned to France in the summer of 1918. Before they could receive combat zone orders, the war ended. In the spring of 1919 Kerr returned home to Ada. He remained in the officers reserve corps holding the rank of captain in the field artillery in the Oklahoma National Guard. In 1925 he was elected Oklahoma State Commander, being the youngest commander in the United States.

A brief attempt at starting a produce business was quickly ended when a fire destroyed the enterprise. Kerr changed directions to deal with a large debt and pursued a new career in law. He became an apprentice in the law office of John F. McKeel, a local judge. For several years Kerr studied to take the state bar examination. During this time he courted his former produce business partner's sister, Reba

Shelton. They were married on December 5, 1919. In 1922, Kerr passed the state bar exam and opened a law office in Ada along with two partners. He began a lifelong involvement with civic interests and activities. He also followed in his father's example of interest in active leadership in the local Baptist church. Kerr taught a Sunday School class and grew in his abilities and reputation as a good speaker. His hopes and dreams were challenged in February, 1924, when his wife, Reba, and their firstborn child died in childbirth.

Even with the tragedy Kerr never lost confidence in his hopes and dreams. A young woman from Tulsa, Grayce Breene, came to Ada to visit her sister. She met Kerr on a tennis court and they began an immediate, serious relationship. On their third date Kerr stated his intention to marry her. They were married on December 26, 1925. Soon after the wedding Kerr accepted an attorney's position with his sister's husband, James L. Anderson. Anderson was an oil drilling contractor who convinced Kerr to join in a partnership. Fortune smiled on both as they began to drill wells in Oklahoma City. Many wells yeilded great oil production in what became known as the Oklahoma City oil basin. Anderson retired in 1936 and a former geologist for the Phillips Petroleum Company, Dean A. McGee, became Kerr's new partner. The lucrative wells provided great fortunes for both men. The company's net worth in 1942 was $7 million. In 1946, McGee became executive vice-president and with Kerr they formed the Kerr-McGee Oil Industries, Incorporated. By 1959 the company's assets exceeded $200 million. The growing oil income allowed Kerr the time and re-sources to pursue his continued interest in civic activities. In 1932, he moved his family to Oklahoma City. The state capitol setting allowed Kerr to immerse himself in the state's Democratic party activities. He was an effective fundraiser aiding in the election of Ernest W. McFarland as governor in 1934 and Leon C. Phillips in 1938. His wide support and respect in the state won his election to the post of Democratic commit-teeman for Oklahoma in 1940. This post allowed him recognition and involvement on a national level.

The 1940 election was a turning point in Oklahoma politics. Kerr was a strong supporter of Franklin D. Roosevelt at the Democratic Convention in Chicago. Governor Phillips did not support a third term or favor the New Deal program. The two men openly clashed and each carried a sizeable portion of the state's delegates to the conven-tion. The split between the two men developed immediately into a strong division in the state's Democratic party. The two would become very bitter political enemies with the fight coming to a head in the 1942 governor's campaign. Although Phillips could not succeed himself as governor, he backed former congressman Gomer Smith as his successor. On April 13, 1942, Kerr announced his candidacy. A very bitter campaign followed for the Democratic party nomination for governor. Kerr narrowly won the primary race by 10,500 votes over Smith. In the general campaign, Governor Phillips supported the Republican candidate, William J. Otjen. With a still-divided party, Kerr won the general election by a narrow margin. With only 400,000 votes cast, Kerr received 16,000 more votes than his opponent. Otjen contested the election results taking his plea to the Oklahoma State Court which found no justification for his suit and declared Kerr the winner.

In addition to business and political offices, Kerr was active in his local church and Baptist denominational offices. Above his regular tithe to Oklahoma City First Baptist Church, Kerr funded a dormitory for Oklahoma Baptist University in Shawnee, Oklahoma. He also "contributed to a limitless number of charities associated with a variety of religious faiths." He served as president of the Baptist General Convention of Oklahoma and vice president of the Southern Baptist Convention. He was president of the Oklahoma Baptist Children's Home helping to raise a half million dollars. Kerr also served on the board of trustees for Oklahoma Baptist University. He delivered the major address for the Southern Baptist Convention in 1955.

Dreams for Oklahoma

On January 11, 1943, Robert Samuel Kerr became the 18th governor of Oklahoma, the first Oklahoma-born governor. Kerr immediately developed a leadership style that found effectiveness in the state legislature. The Democrats were dominant in the state house and senate. Kerr established a close, personal working relationship with the state leadership. He "preferred to meet in quiet conferences with the leaders of the legislature rather to resort to threats or use patronage to gain their support." This generated positive cooperation on most important state issues. This leadership style paralleled Holloway's style as a neutral and bipartisan governor and Bennett's style as a college president adept at building effective relationships.

Retiring the state's accumulated debt of more than $36 million was Kerr's first priority. He stated publicly that "As long as I am

Governor every effort will be made to *pay* debts and not *create* them." He led in designating surplus budget funds to go toward debt reduction. He led the state legislature in establishing the Oklahoma School Bond Retirement Fund which would purchase over $5 million in bonds. Kerr set the example for cutting expenditures in his own executive actions. He cut executive and security employees and refused the services of a personal bodyguard. These actions reflected the chief goal of frugality and economic stability which paralleled the activities of Holloway and Bennett as leaders. Kerr also refused to cut taxes despite the strong business and private interest pressures. Through all of these measures, the state debt was retired in 1945.

Several other significant amendments to the Oklahoma Constitution were supported by Kerr. He led in the creation of a non-partisan Oklahoma Pardon and Parole Board, limiting the governor's unrestricted power to deal with clemency appeals. He also proposed creation of a non-partisan board of regents for Oklahoma A & M College and the University of Oklahoma. In July, 1944, voters approved both legislative measures. Kerr also signed a measure allowing for absentee voting because of the wartime military personnel being away.

With World War II coming to a victorious conclusion, Kerr set out a program of postwar development for Oklahoma. His plans centered on "increased funds for support of public schools, for construction of roads, for improvement of public health services, and for tax incentives for individuals and industries." After a series of discussions and compromises, the state legislature allotted $15.6 million a year for the next two years. This appropriation almost doubled the amount made available for public education by the previous legislature. Kerr maintained a consistent salary scale for teachers in Oklahoma, a rarity from past gubernatorial leadership.

Kerr's efforts to balance the budget required some tough actions to increase state revenues. He proposed a two-cent-per-gallon, gas tax that would raise $7 million. The legislature also approved an increased tax on auto licenses, which would raise $500,000 a year. The most controversial proposal was a big increase, $5 per barrel, in the tax on beer. There were strong attacks against Kerr who was a teetotaler. His reply was "There is not a beer drinker who has to drink the slop if he doesn't want to pay the tax." Kerr's economic goal and efforts regarding the state budget deficit were accomplished in January 1947 when he left office. He proclaimed that "for the first time since Statehood, no indebtedness of any kind was outstanding against the State of Oklahoma..."

Kerr's personal loyalties, even as governor, brought criticism of the use of his office. The previous governor, Leon C. Phillips, in December of 1942, had "filed a lawsuit on behalf of the people of Oklahoma that charged thirty-three individuals and textbook firms with defrauding the state of over $5.3 million in the selection of books for the public schools." One of the more prominent individuals named in the lawsuit was Henry Garland Bennett, president of Oklahoma A & M College, the close personal friend of Kerr and Holloway. It is interesting to note that the charges were made only one month after Phillips had lost in his influence to stop the election of Kerr to the governorship. Specific charges against Henry Bennett were strong. The increased costs in textbooks authored by Bennett were due to text changes and updates. No grounds for charges were discovered. Ten percent of the textbook sales were supposed to go to the William H. Murray Education Foundation. Supposedly Bennett failed to deposit royalty sales with the Murray Education Foundation. The lawsuit dragged on slowly. Kerr, as governor, pressed for a legislative investigation. An appointed committee continued to act very slowly in its investigation. A county grand jury finally convened in Tulsa and indicted Henry Bennett on charges of conspiracy. With the trial in progress, Kerr publicly expressed his support of Bennett. Kerr received strong criticism from his political enemies for his commitment to his personal friend. In December of 1943, Judge Bower Broaddus dismissed the case against Bennett due to the "expiration of the statute of limitations." Upon appeal, the case against Bennett was heard in the federal circuit court in Oklahoma City. In May, 1944 they agreed with Judge Broaddus and dismissed the case against Henry Bennett.

It seems there has been much speculation as to the charges against Bennett and the public support of Kerr as governor. They shared a long-time friendship of mutual support and admiration. They had joined forces in going against former Governor Phillips, who maintained a vendetta against both of them. There were also forces in the state that were very anti-Henry Bennett in his long tenure as Oklahoma A & M College president. Those political enemies of Kerr saw an opportunity to discredit a popular governor. Whether Bennett was actually guilty of the charges has never been substantiated. There were others indicted in what became known as the "Oklahoma textbook scandal," who received a more severe public trial. Alvin B. Crable was the Oklahoma superintendent of public instruction. He was a close friend of Henry Bennett and Governor Kerr. Even though he was found not chargeable by the state legislature early on, pressures continued to mount evidence of complicity. Crable was accused with J. T. Daniel, earlier speaker of the house, and Howard B. Drake, an executive appointee at the same time, of receiving $60,000 in bribes from the textbook publishers. After a very contentious three days of debate in the house chambers, a close vote favored Crable and the others. Although the vote eliminated further investigations, the stigma of guilt and the division created would continue for many years ahead.

Robert Kerr's effectiveness and national recognition came with the March, 1944 special election in Oklahoma for the vacated seat of representative from the second congressional district. Both political parties garnered support for their candidates from within the state and from national party leadership. The Republicans supported E. O. Clark, an anti-New Dealer. The Democrats, who had been losing ground in the national House majority, nominated William G. Stigler, a strong New Dealer. Neighboring anti-New Dealers and pro-New Dealer senators came to Oklahoma to lend their support and show the national interest in the election. Kerr mobilized a rally at Muskogee the day before the election. He had invited Alben W. Barkley, then United States senate majority leader, to speak. Kerr acted as the master of ceremonies and spoke strongly in Stigler's support. Kerr's behind the scenes and public activities were effective in Stigler's victory by only 3,700 votes. Kerr's actions caught the attention of Washington as a man of influence and effectiveness.

Kerr's rise in national prominence resulted in an invitation for him to give the keynote address at the1944 Democratic National Convention. With short time to prepare, Kerr invited his friend, Henry Bennett, to help him write his speech. The two worked together at a Minnesota retreat. Kerr also deflected criticism of his time away from the state by paying for his own expenses on these trips. At the Chicago national convention, Robert Kerr was also seriously considered by some as a candidate for vice president on the national ticket. Instead of pushing for the position, Kerr became a strong supporter of Harry S. Truman for the vice-presidential spot. Kerr was also instrumental in breaking up "a coalition of favorite son candidates which enabled Truman to secure the vice-presidential nomination. On July 19, 1944, Kerr gave his keynote speech "before a capacity audience of 25,000 of the party faithful. His speech criticized Thomas Dewey's inexperience and praised Roosevelt's accomplishments. Interrupted by boisterous demonstrations of support, the speech was well received by the highly-enthusiastic audience." This speech, carried on national radio, gave Kerr even higher prominence and recognition in Oklahoma and the nation. Kerr and Bennett worked together as a great team. Both were able to understand their audience and the opposition. Kerr's keen political insights and Bennett's trained and experienced speaking style would combine to ensure a powerful and effective speech.

With the death of President Roosevelt on April 12, 1945, Kerr's national influence with President Truman would continue and grow. Kerr's influence in promoting Truman as vice president was not forgotten. Kerr grew in recognition in his involvement with the national governor's conference. In 1945, he served as a member of the national executive board, presided over the annual meeting of the Southern Governor's Conference planning meeting and chaired the Southern Governor's Conference later that year in Miami, Florida. The meeting was deemed the best ever and credit was given to Kerr for "his outgoing personality and organizational ability." It was an even more notable accomplishment considering he represented a comparatively poorer state in the shadow of the eastern establishment and neighboring Texan political leadership.

Supporter of National Dreams

Kerr's departure from the governor's office in January, 1947, allowed him to return to duties as a principal officer at Kerr-McGee oil industries. It also gave him the time to plan his campaign for the United States Senate. The campaign evolved into a repeat of the vicious gubernatorial campaign six years earlier. He faced his previous foe, Gomer Smith. The campaign revolved around Kerr's support of the current president and the civil rights initiatives. Kerr ran on the positive issue in his slogan, "Land, Wood, and Water." He handily defeated Gomer Smith in the July, 1948 primary election. Kerr then easily defeated his Republican opponent, Ross Rizley, becoming the first Oklahoma governor to become a United States senator. The state would honor him two more times in senate campaigns in 1954 and 1960.

Kerr's influence with the new Truman administration was also instrumental in his support for Oklahoma State A & M president, Henry G. Bennett, to be named as director of the Point Four program in 1950. Kerr was well aware of Bennett's ability and Truman's desire for an outsider to be committed to Truman's dream for the program. It is also certain that Kerr helped Bennett in his effort to gain much-needed approval and congressional funding for the program.

In the early fall of 1955, the Oklahoma City Chamber of Commerce created the Frontiers of Science Foundation of Oklahoma. Truman's former director of the budget and undersecretary of state, James E. Webb, was elected as president of the organization. Phil Bennett, Henry Bennett's son, was elected as a board member. The need to improve the state's education and industry was envisioned through the sciences. Kerr was actively interested and involved in the process of this organization. Other national leaders were watching with interest. The launch of Sputnik by the Russians in 1957 prompted almost panicked interest in science education and technology. The Frontiers of Science Foundation now became of great national interest in spurring competition with the Soviet space program. Kerr was personally involved as a senator and an Oklahoman. He was also the chairman of the Senate Aeronautics and Space Sciences Committee. He made numerous visits to the research centers and consulted with James Webb regularly. Kerr was instrumental in the passage of the 1958 National Aeronautics Space and Administration Act.

Kerr's primary task as senator was to work aggressively for flood control and river navigation projects. Previously, as governor, he had actively promoted these projects with national leaders, especially after the flood of 1943. As early as November, 1927, he had appeared before the United States House of Representatives Committee on Flood Control. This encouraged the direction of the Army Corps of Engineers to "prepare a flood control plan for the Mississippi River Valley System, which included the Arkansas River basin." With delays because of World War II expenses, in July, 1946, Congress approved $55 million for "multipurpose development of the Arkansas River and its tributaries in the states of Arkansas and Oklahoma." Kerr's position in the senate as chairman of the Senate Rivers and Harbors Committee, senior Democrat on the Public Works Committee, and as a member of the Senate Appropriations Committee, helped to ensure the progress for completion of the Arkansas River navigation projects.

Kerr, while maintaining a growing influence in the Senate, also gained a reputation for his strong parochialism for Oklahoma interests. He was described by his colleagues as "a strong debater who overwhelmed opponents with his passion and his mastery of details." The Saturday Evening Post, April 9, 1949, nicknamed him "the big boom from Oklahoma: the richest—and loudest—man in the United States Senate." In 1950 Kerr attempted to pass deregulation of natural gas for independent producers. Truman vetoed the bill in spite of its personal benefit to Kerr because "it was not in the public interest." But in 1951, when Truman fired the popular General MacArthur, Robert Kerr was the sole Democratic senator to come to Truman's defense. This was noted and deeply appreciated by Truman.

Henry Bennett's tragic death was a great personal loss for Kerr. He was asked to deliver a eulogy for Dr. and Mrs. Bennett at the funeral service in Stillwater, Oklahoma, on January 5, 1952. Kerr was moved as he shared his thoughts concerning his friend and ally.

> I saw him before a great committee of the Senate. It was a fine and yet as tough a committee as I ever saw. Yet he captivated its members and won their unanimous support. I saw him with the President of the United States. He showed the President that he knew as much about the President's Program and what it could do as the President did himself. I saw him with the Secretary of State and his great staff of able and vigorous men. In a little while they learned that he knew as much or more of the job they had given him to do than they did. I talked with him before he started and as he would return from his trips abroad to South America, or Africa or Asia. Always he was the same dynamic, confident, courageous, yet humble friend. He was just as kind and humble, yet just as forthright and vigorous as when he was teaching in a county school or serving as Superintendent of the schools of Choctaw County. He knew he had come from the soil and no matter how far he traveled he never left it nor did he ever lose its undiminished energy and power.

Kerr sought unsuccessfully in 1952 to win the Democratic nomination for the presidency. In President Truman's *Memoirs*, an observation was made regarding Truman's feelings toward Robert Kerr. Truman wrote:

> Bob Kerr demonstrated that as governor and as senator he possessed administrative and legislative ability of high order. But his background of representing the oil and gas interests in the Senate

made him ineligible in my opinion. I have always felt that any man who goes either to the Senate or the House to represent a special interest in his own state and who sponsors legislation to help that special interest forfeits any claim to national leadership in the Democratic party. Historically, the Democratic party is not a special interest party.

Kerr's strong leadership helped to provide assurance in key programs such as the North Atlantic Treaty Organization, the Marshall Plan, military aid to allies, the Point Four program, the Mutual Security Program, the Reconstruction Finance Corporation and effective antitrust laws and consumer price-gouging controls. Although Kerr personally profited from the natural resources in Oklahoma, he remained the strongest proponent of conservation of natural resources.

President Kennedy's effort to pass the creation of Medicare was defeated because of Kerr's opposition. The Wall Street Journal, January 3, 1963, explained the relationship between Robert Kerr and Kennedy regarding legislation: "Mr. Kennedy asked; Mr. Kerr decided." Kerr became chairman of the Senate Aeronautics and Space Sciences Committee. He was able, with his threats of a filibuster, to pass a satellite communications bill. In 1962, he used his strong influence to get his friend and Oklahoma Kerr-McGee officer, James E. Webb, appointed as the second director of the National Space and Aeronautics Administration (NASA). He would become NASA's and Webb's strongest supporter in congress. His power and influence in the Senate became legendary. Senator Paul H. Douglas gave him the title of the "uncrowned king of the senate."

His total senate career was based on his campaign of "Land, Wood, and Water." He claimed the greatest pride in his leadership in the conservation of natural resources, especially in Oklahoma. A month before his death, Kerr "rededicated himself to his goals for his state. As he traveled by plane to his home, he said, 'If I live ten more years in this job, there won't be a muddy stream left in Oklahoma.'"

On December 18, 1962, Senator Kerr suffered a severe heart attack. He was admitted to the Bethesda Hospital in Washington, D. C. He was expected to make a full recovery. On January 1, 1963, he died instantly of a massive heart attack. The state and the nation were in shock. His body laid in state at the Oklahoma City state capitol on January 3. On January 4 the funeral was held at the Rose Hill Mausoleum. In attendance was President John F. Kennedy, Vice-President

Lyndon B. Johnson, congressional colleagues and his family. His body was eventually taken to the original place of his birth two miles southeast of Ada, Oklahoma, and placed in "a large but not elaborate stone vault."

Robert Kerr, as a dreamer, envisioned much for his beloved state and his own career. He established financial stability for a heavily-indebted state as governor. He promoted and achieved numerous long-term projects for his state and its citizens. There is the strong suggestion that had Robert Kerr lived longer, the headquarters of NASA might have been located in Burns Flat, then home of the longest air runway in the United States. He supported his fellow dreamers unapologetically in their struggles and sought their career advancements.

Chapter Four

Harry S. Truman

A fellow commoner with dreams in common

Of all the fellow dreamers, there has been more written with detailed history of Harry S. Truman than the others combined. This chapter will look at the interrelationships between Truman and the fellow dreamers. As powerful as Truman was as president, he still needed the cooperative support and assistance of these men and their insights. There are several interesting parallels of Truman's background and those of men like Henry Bennett, William Holloway and Robert Kerr. They were all common men of the land. They came from very modest farm families in the middle of America. They came from religious families with strong Christian ethics. They all had experienced some business and investment failures. They all dreamed dreams far beyond their beginning stations in life. They were politically active and valued education. They had a universal love for people.

Background of a Dreamer

Harry S. Truman was born May 8, 1884, to John and Margaret Truman, in Lamar, Missouri. His father was a livestock trader who struggled to make a modest living for his family. His mother was an industrious housewife with a strong appreciation for the arts and a strong dedication to the Christian faith. Truman grew up a "momma's boy" but struggled to gain the respect of his father. As a young man, Truman worked in the fields and with the farm animals. He experienced the joys of a good harvest and the devastation of cruel, weather-related failures. He became aware of the dependency on agricultural production and the great economic challenges facing the farm families. Like

Henry Bennett and Robert Kerr, Truman grew up knowing the hard labor and risks of working the land.

Truman grew up with experiences in both the Baptist and Presbyterian churches. He identified himself as a "lightfoot Baptist." His dedication and active membership did not appear to be as strong as those of Henry Bennett, William Holloway and Robert Kerr. Both Bennett and Holloway were children of active Baptist preachers while Kerr's father was an active Sunday School teacher. Bennett and Kerr would become dedicated Sunday School teachers in their local Baptist churches. Bennett and Kerr would also become actively involved with Baptist denominational affairs and organization. Truman would be inclined to remain happily removed from the denominational politics.

Truman, as the other dreamers, would become involved in additional business away from the farm to assist with the limited family income. He experienced early employment as a drug store custodian, mailroom clerk, railroad construction crew timekeeper, as well as various positions in the banking business. Bennett experienced employment as a laundry and grocery deliverer, rural postal carrier and a book salesman. Kerr worked briefly at a cement plant, but principally stayed active working on the farm.

All four men were actively involved in local, state and national politics. All were committed Democrats and participated consistently in elections. Bennett would never run for a political office, but he was actively involved in his support for favored candidates. Truman, Holloway and Kerr knew the joys and risks of running for local and state offices. Holloway ran for Oklahoma state representative, state senator and lieutenant governor. His rise to governorship was a result of another impeachment. Kerr ran for Oklahoma governor and senator. He was unsuccessful in his attempts to run for national offices. Truman ran for county offices and Missouri state senator. He lost his attempt to run for U. S. representative because of his refusal to accept the demands of the Ku Klux Klan. Truman, alone, would experience the rare privilege of running for national office.

Truman, Holloway and Kerr knew the discipline of military service. Holloway and Kerr enlisted in the military because of World War I. Both were deployed for combat activity but the war ended before they saw combat action. Bennett never became active in the military, although his leadership in the education field would provide training and education for thousands of people in the military. Truman desired training at West Point but was denied because of his poor eyesight. He was able to join a local national guard unit that had lower standards for eyesight. As World War I began and the nation prepared for combat, National Guard units were transformed into the mobilized armed services. Truman was able to sneak his way into the military ranks. He eventually commanded the Battery D of the 2nd Battalion, 129th Field Artillery that saw fierce action in France.

All four men valued the need for higher education. Bennett, Holloway and Kerr achieved advanced degrees in education and worked many years as educators. It is interesting that Truman would be the one who did not go on to achieve a college education. In his home and at high school reading was promoted and he had access to great literary works. Truman continued to be self-educated and never loss his thirst for learning.

Oklahoma provided a common link for Henry Bennett, William Holloway, Robert Kerr, Harry Truman, Haile Selassie and James Webb. Bennett improved education in the state as a county superintendent and long-term president of two state colleges. Holloway taught in public schools, successfully ran in state politics and practiced law. Kerr was a successful businessman and successfully ran for office in state politics. Truman had several adventures in the state in natural resource speculations and military training. Emperor Haile Selassie honored the state with his visit in 1954. Webb worked for the Kerr/McGee company and directed the important Oklahoma Frontiers of Science program.

Although Truman worked hard on the family farm, he was constantly drawn to other areas of interest. He found limited success in his non-agricultural, business ventures. There may have been another interest drawing Truman away from the family farm. That was his growing attraction to Bess Wallace. At those times when Truman seemed to be settled comfortably in business ventures, the family farm demanded his attention. Crop failures, family illnesses and deaths seemed to keep drawing Truman back to the farm. He would be in his late thirties before he was finally able to escape the demands of the farm and live his own life.

His poor eyesight caused a limitation in the normal physical pursuits of other youth, but allowed him to explore the world of literary and artistic appreciation. Even with limitations due to the demands of the farm, his eyesight and family finances, Truman never lost sight of his personal dreams. When his eyesight prevented him from achieving an education at West Point, he never lost sight of the dream of serving his country through the military. Even when Bess's family disapproved of her interest in Truman— she was thought to be marrying down— he never lost sight of his dream regarding their relationship. When Truman experienced failure in business interests in Oklahoma and in Kansas City, he continued his dream for success. That sense of keeping the dreams in spite of obstacles would carry him throughout his life, even in the presidency.

Truman's contact with the fellow dreamers may have been as early as his ventures in Oklahoma mineral speculations. In mid-1916 Truman invested with others in a zinc mine at Commerce, Oklahoma, in the northeast corner of the state. It was 192 miles from the family farm in Grandview, Missouri. He was a business partner with David Morgan and Jerry Culbertson. Truman's mother and uncle also invested in the mine speculation. This added to the high sense of personal responsibility for him in the success of the venture. The mine did not provide the great profits anticipated. Truman worked hard as overseer and even worked as night watchman to save on expenses. His two partners were not as committed and assisted little in the mine operations. In September, 1916, the mine closed leaving all of them with their investments lost. The Bennett family recalled that Vera Bennett's father had invested in the mine. The investors were called to a meeting to discuss the failure. The Bennett family recalled that Henry Bennett went with Vera's father to those meetings. They very possibly could have met a young Harry Truman who was serving as the mine operator and bookkeeper. The Bennett family also indicated that Kerr may have invested in the mining venture.

There is also some question of Truman's encounter with the fellow dreamers during his military training at Camp Doniphan at Fort Sill in Lawton, Oklahoma. Nothing can be confirmed by any of the families.

Political Dreams

Other early contacts with Truman and the fellow dreamers were more likely due to their common political interests. Bennett, Holloway and Kerr were active in local, state and national Democratic activities. It is very likely that there were encounters at political rallies and conventions. It is certain that Bennett and Kerr would have encountered Truman at the 1944 Democratic National Convention. Kerr's strong support of Truman as the Democratic vice-presidential nominee in 1946 established an important relationship between the two men.

When Truman became president, there were numerous encounters between the fellow dreamers. Kerr, serving as Oklahoma senator, would meet with Truman to discuss legislative and international matters. James Webb was appointed as the director of the powerful Budget Bureau and worked daily with Truman and certainly with Senator Kerr. Bennett had met on two occasions with Truman before Bennett's appointment as Point Four director. He met Truman in the Oval Office February 4, 1948 with Mr. Elmer Harber, who was on the Oklahoma A & M Board of Regents. On January 10, 1950, Bennett, accompanied by Senator Kerr, met again in the Oval Office with Truman to discuss his international trips and observations.

International Dreams

With Truman's surprising election victory in 1948, all areas of national politics were caught off guard. It was also a time of change within the administration's organizational structure. The international situation was challenging because of human suffering in war-ravaged countries. Communist aggression was also of paramount concern to the free world leadership. The U. S. State Department was undergoing change with General Marshall's declining health. Truman's Budget Bureau Director, James Webb, was moved to the State Department as undersecretary of state. Truman wanted his 1949 Inaugural Address to send a message of international help and warning. Truman had seen first hand as president the ravages of war in Europe. He made a point to tour a destroyed Germany at the Potsdam Conference. With State Department infighting trying to protect existing but inadequate programs, there was very little assistance in trying to meet Truman's proposed international policies. Inclusion of the fourth point in Truman's 1949 inaugural address came about with secretive and dedicated assistance from Benjamin Hardy. After the 1949 inaugural address, there were strong, favorable reactions especially to the fourth point. Truman now had the monumental task of getting the program operable. It needed to be approved in Congress, accepted in the State Department and adequately funded and staffed. In all of these tasks, it would be Kerr and Webb who provided the necessary guidance.

In June, 1950, a national meeting of the National Education Association (NEA) in Washington, D. C. was asked to examine the Point Four program, as envisioned by Truman. It was carefully analyzed with recommendations for its purpose and staffing. The organization saw Point Four as an education program, requiring an educator as its leader instead of a career, State Department person. All of the pieces were coming together to unite many of these fellow dreamers. The recommendations of the NEA, the recommendations of Kerr and Webb, and Truman's previous personal meetings, led Truman to choose Henry Bennett as the Point Four director. It is significant that Truman bypassed the ivy leaguers and chose an outsider, but one with the practical experience with innovations in agricultural technology that would be needed. It was Webb who actually made the telephone call to Bennett asking him to meet with Truman to discuss the position. They met in the Oval Office with Truman on November 14, 1950. Bennett accepted the position with the pending approval of a leave from Oklahoma A & M College, to be supported by the board of regents.

With the program narrowly approved by Congress and a director appointed, there remained the challenges of getting the program accepted by the State Department as well as acquiring adequate funding and quality staffing. Truman's intervention forced the State Department acceptance along with some indirect assistance by Webb. Bennett's appearance and style before Congress enabled the program to gain more than adequate congressional funding with the assistance of Kerr.

Truman's attitude toward the State Department was best communicated to his former business partner, David Morgan, in a letter dated January 28, 1952.

> The State Department is a peculiar organization, made up principally of extremely bright people who made tremendous college marks but who had very little association with actual people down to the ground. They are clannish and snooty and sometimes I feel like firing the whole bunch but it requires a tremendous amount of education to accomplish the purposes for which the State Department is set up. In a great many key places I have men of common sense and we are improving the situation right along.

> The present Secretary of State is one of the best that has ever been in office, but on lower levels we still have the career men who

have been taken out of college without any experience with the common people.

Bennett's first selection on his staff was Benjamin Hardy. He was certainly made aware of Hardy's unselfish contributions to the program's origin. Hardy was appointed as an associate advisor with public relations responsibilities. Hardy's effectiveness in this professional area would be motivated by his intense interest in seeing the program succeed. Hardy provided great assistance to Bennett in writing speeches and press releases explaining the program's purposes and accomplishments. He also provided a good link with the State Department leadership, still suspicious of the program and of Bennett as an outsider. Bennett enlisted others from the Department of Agriculture, the Interior Department, the Treasury, the Budget Bureau, Public Health, educational institutions and other State Department international programs being operated less effectively.

As Bennett began his leadership in developing this new bold program, he traveled widely becoming very much a hands-on director. He evaluated needs, national leadership and necessary personnel. After his travels, he often returned to Washington, D. C. to consult with key leaders. He met with Kerr, State Department personnel and with Truman. The Truman oval office records indicate five occasions where Bennett consulted with Truman. His first visit as Point Four director with Truman was on January 1, 1951, prior to his extended trip to Central and South America. He met the president along with Nelson Rockefeller. On April 10 and 18, 1951, he met with Truman and Undersecretary of State Webb to report on his trips. He gave the president a report of the Point Four activities on October 24, 1951. His last visit with Truman was in the Rose Garden on November 20, 1951, accompanied by 51 delegates and 20 trainees from the World Land Tenure Conference, which represented 38 countries.

Truman was facing tremendous opposition at home from a number of sources. On April 10, 1951, Truman fired General Douglas MacArthur from his Far Eastern military command. At that time, the national polls indicated a 69% approval for MacArthur. At the same time, Joseph MacCarthy was publicly attacking Truman administration officials as being part of a communist conspiracy. The Korean War was going badly with great loss of American soldiers and support at home.

Truman was also facing personal pressures. On November 1, 1950, two Puerto Rican nationalists attempted to assassinate Truman outside of the Blair house. On December 5, 1950, Truman's longtime friend, Charlie Ross, advisor and press secretary, died at his White House desk. When Truman made the announcement, he broke down and left in tears. That same evening he and Bess attended daughter Margaret's concert at Constitution Hall. The next day, *Washington Post* music critic Paul Hume panned the performance and later received the harsh letter of attack from Truman. Other great losses for Truman were the deaths of Henry Bennett and Benjamin Hardy on December 22, 1951. His public response was personal and emotional. He knew that besides the loss of valued friendships was the loss of effective leadership for his promising international assistance program. Another aspect of the tragedy was losing the continuing effectiveness of fulfilling the international, humanitarian dreams of Truman, Bennett and Hardy. Truman would realize that he alone could not fulfill these dreams—it took a cooperative effort of the combined dreams and talents of committed leaders.

At a luncheon in Cincinnati in 1959, Stanley Andrews, who followed Bennett as Point Four director, met with Truman. He recounted:

> So I went over and I was the last person to get in and I had to walk right in front of the speaker's platform. Charlie Taft was presiding, he's from Cincinnati. And I had to walk by to get the last seat there was in the room and just as I walked by, President Truman was looking at some papers and I, just in passing by, I said, "Hello, Mr. President," or something like that and I didn't even stop. "Hey!" he said, "Where the hell have you been?" or something to that effect. And he startled me you see. And then right off the bat, he said, "Why did Henry Bennett go to Iran and get killed?" I said, "Mr. President, I've always felt guilty about that. I sort of talked him into going up there." "Well," he said, "I knew he was going, but I told him not to ride on one of those blankety, blank airlines." And he said, "Why couldn't he have gone some other way?"

When Truman left office in early 1953, things changed dramatically in international relationships and foreign policy. Without the voices and representation of Bennett and Hardy, it was difficult for Truman to expedite his international ideals. The high ideals of the Truman Point Four program were quickly replaced by the negative perceptions of the "ugly American" foreign policy. Truman remained a strong influence and sounding board for many of the Washington leaders. He would campaign for Democratic candidates such as Robert Kerr. He would have great influence in the Kennedy/Johnson administrations. He would favor the appointment of James Webb as NASA's second administrator.

People who knew Truman wrote of his dreams and unselfish desires to help all peoples of the world. Ken Hechler, an administrative aid in Truman White House office, noted "If I had to pick Mr. Truman's one trait that made me proudest of all to work for him, it was that he never lost the common touch and was determined to use the awesome power of the president to help bring peace and justice to average people all over the world." The day after Truman died, Mary McGrory, wrote a tribute to him in the *Washington Star*. She wrote that "He was not a hero or a magician or a chess player, or an obsession. He was a certifiable member of the human race, direct, fallible, and unexpectedly wise when it counted." She continued:

> He did not require to be loved. He did not expect to be followed blindly. Congressional opposition never struck him as subversive, nor did he regard his critics as traitors. He never whined.

> He walked around Washington every morning—it was safe then. He met frequently with reporters as a matter of course, and did not blame them for his failures. He did not use the office as a club or a shield, or a hiding place. He worked at it…He said he lived by the Bible and history. So armed, he proved that the ordinary American is capable of grandeur. And that a President can be a human being…

Many years after Truman's death, other authors would rediscover the dreams and impact of this great man. David McCullough, in his wonderful biography of Truman, summarized that

> Ambitious by nature, he was never torn by ambition, never tried to appear as something he was not. He stood for common sense, common decency. He spoke the common tongue. As much as any president since Lincoln, he brought to the highest office the language and values of the common American people. He held to the old guidelines: work hard, do your best, speak the truth, assume no airs, trust in God, have no fear. Yet he was not and had never been a simple, ordinary man…He was the kind of president the founding fathers had in mind for the country.

Robert Ferrell, in his biography of Truman, concluded in similar expressions that

> Harry Truman was a farm-boy President who had come up the hard way through the army and through years as a local official...he had a reserve of salty language, and a ready wit. He could say things that were too quotable. Sophisticates saw him as gauche and uninstructed; they were embarrassed by a President who would play the piano in public—and so obviously enjoy himself. Now his owlish spectacles and rumpled suits, his simple habits and fatherly pride, his passion for history, his pungent humor, his love for Bess all are part of a charm that reminds us that a good President and a good person can be one."

In every list ranking the American presidents in order of importance and quality, Truman is nearly always ranked in the top ten. He was content to let history record his place and the significance of his decisions as president. His decisions as president were certainly significant: commanding and ending a world war, dropping the first and second atomic bombs, maintaining a war and peace time national economy, saving a starving Europe from destruction, stopping communist aggression in Europe, supporting a United Nations organization, commanding a war in Korea, organizing a technical assistance program to help underdeveloped countries of the world, defending his administration leaders of false charges, integrating the American armed services and just ignoring public opinion polls and doing what he felt was right.

Truman, with the other fellow dreamers he encountered, found deep roots in the land, the common people and a higher purpose for existence than personal wealth or power. He loved his country and all its citizens. He had great dreams for the peoples of the world—especially the suffering and uneducated. His association with these fellow dreamers provided avenues for the practical application of his dreams.

Chapter Five

Haile Selassie

An international ally with national dreams

It may seem strange that Haile Selassie would be included in this list of "fellow dreamers," but there is an interrelationship with Bennett and the convergence of their dreams that qualifies his inclusion. Where Bennett had dreams of international assistance, Selassie sought such help in achieving the dreams he had for the nation of Ethiopia. Both men had dreams of making a quality education available for all people that would provide the tools for improving the food production, health and technological advances in their states. Bennett's association with Selaissie developed into a mutually respectful alliance which allowed for great realization of their convergent ideas.

Background of a Dreamer

Haile Selassie was born in 1892 in Ethiopia with the birth name of Tafari Makonnen. This was a crucial time in Ethiopia's history. The country had been given European approval to be under Italian influence. The country's rich agricultural potential and cultural accomplishments were desired by Italy in its expansions. Emperor Menelik II dispelled Italian control and sought to rule his country as a sovereign nation. Though there were several conflicts, the country maintained its sovereignty. By the 1900s, Ethiopia was recognized as a sovereign nation by the European colonial powers.

Tafari Makonnen married Wayzaro Menen, the granddaughter of Emperor Menelik, in 1911. In doing so, he became a prince (Ras). There was great dissatisfaction with the Emperor's grandson, Lij Yasu, who was assumed to inherit the throne. Lij Yasu was unreliable and disliked as a leader in the country. The political Christian majority favored the Emperor's new son-in-law. The people had noticed that Makonnen had developed progressive leadership and humanitarian concerns. In 1917 Makonnen was named regent and heir to the throne. For the next thirteen years Makonnen became active as an official representative of the country. He sought to promote Ethiopia as a valuable ally to the other countries. He was the first Ethiopian ruler to travel abroad visiting the European capitols. During these travels Tafari took note of the modernization in the cities of Europe and compared them to the backward conditions in Ethiopia. He returned from his travels with dreams to improve the lot of his people and his country. He immediately began to take steps to improve the democratic political processes in order for them to be more in line with European models. He led in progressive improvements in education and social services within the country. In 1919 he applied for membership in the League of Nations. His request was denied because of Ethiopia's active practice of slavery. Working with Empress Zauditu, slavery was abolished and the country was accepted unanimously into the League of Nations in 1923. This further solidified Ethiopia as a free and sovereign nation.

At this time, the Italian government under Benito Mussolini began to emphasize Italian dominance of the African region, threatening Ethiopia's sovereignty. Although Makonnen promoted a twenty-year treaty of friendship with Italy, Mussolini still sought dominance of Ethiopian territories for strategic purposes. The dreams of Makonnen represented an immanent clash with the desire for control by Mussolini.

Dreams and Challenges of a National Leader

In November of 1930, Empress Zauditu died and Makonnen became the official Emperor of Ethiopia assuming full kingship. He was the 111th emperor in the line of King Solomon. He took the name of Haile Selassie which means "Might of the Trinity." He began to unify national control through establishing Ethiopia's first constitution. He wanted to move the governance from the control of other princes to his own bloodline. There were several princes who rebelled but were defeated until unity was completed by 1934. During this time the emperor sought to make major improvements in the country's welfare. He banned the illegal sale of arms in Ethiopia. He established the right to procure arms for the country's self-defense. The Bank of Ethiopia was established in

1931. At that time Ethiopian currency was introduced. He began an aggressive campaign of building schools, supporting newspapers, and providing modernized utility services for the public.

Although Selassie worked to develop and improve his country through sovereign actions, Mussolini began to work toward his own control of the country. When internal conflicts and even battles occurred, it appeared as though international indifference and League of Nations ineffectiveness gave Mussolini an open door for further hostilities toward Ethiopia. In October of 1935 Italy invaded Ethiopia. Although the League of Nations condemned Italy, no action was taken. Over a period of seven months, the Ethiopian forces were beaten back by Mussolini's superior military and the use of chemical weapons. Italy had gained control of Somaliland to the south of Ethiopia and control of Eritrea to the north. On May 2, 1936, Emperor Haile Selassie was forced into exile in Great Britain.

Selassie's departure from Ethiopia raised some criticism for not continuing the country's tradition of warring emperors. He gave an impassioned speech to the League of Nations on June 30, 1936. It was the first time that the head of a nation addressed the League and its delegates. The Emperor would explain why in his remarks.

> It is in order to denounce to the civilized world the tortures inflicted upon the Ethiopian people that I resolved to come to Geneva. None other than myself and my brave companions in arms could bring the League of Nations the undeniable proof. The appeals of my delegates addressed to the League of Nations had remained without any answer; my delegates had not been witnesses. That is why I decided to come myself to bear witness against the crime perpetrated against my people and give Europe a warning of doom that awaits, if it should bow before the accomplished fact.

The appearance and speech produced little in the way of actual help but did gain the sympathy and respect of the United States. In spite of Selassie's lobbying and diplomatic efforts, Great Britain and France refused to challenge Italy's claim of Ethiopian possession. Continued clashes occurred in Ethiopia as Mussolini installed a new government and sought to establish political dominance. Selassie's ineffective attempts to gain international support changed with the beginning of World War II when Italy entered on the side of Germany in June, 1940.

Britain now had more motivation to assist the emperor. The remaining loyal forces of Ethiopia continued to endure severe massacres and isolation at the hands of the new, Italian-established government in Ethiopia. In 1940 Selassie moved to Khartoum to more effectively coordinate the revolutionary forces. On May 5, 1941, Selassie was able to re-enter Addis Ababa with the combined forces of Ethiopians, British, South African and African combat forces. Fighting in Ethiopia continued until the beginning of 1942 when Ethiopian and allied forces gained military and political control. As Selassie began to regain his control, he made decisions and took actions without British approval. He took great efforts to maintain personal control of the country. He instituted an unpopular flat tax based on land values. He eliminated external control of the Eastern Orthodox Church by directly appointing the patriarch. Continuing reforms led to a modernization of Ethiopia and a broadened relationship with other world powers. One of the needs was for educational reform to improve agricultural, medical and engineering education.

In 1942 slaveholding was made illegal. In a 1950 interview the emperor stated that "I have three priorities in my country. I first want to expand education. My second ambition is to develop communications. And the third—I want to secure employment for all Ethiopians."

Point Four Dreams

As British control eased, Selassie made new aid relationships with the United States. In early 1950, the emperor invited Dr. Henry Bennett to Ethiopia as "an advisor to Ethiopian educators and agriculturalists on the organization of an agricultural training center along the lines of land-grant colleges." Bennett was recognized as the "dean of land-grant colleges" in the United States. He had past international experiences at the Quebec Conference and in helping West Germany with agricultural recovery after World War II. These credits made Bennett an ideal advisor for an emperor with dreams for his country.

As Bennett toured the country, he saw such great agricultural potential. He made recommendations that were largely accepted by the emperor. He also discussed the possibility of Bennett's Oklahoma A & M College assisting in the plans. The emperor's dreams would be greatly enhanced by Bennett's acceptance as director of the Point Four program. The United States and Ethiopia signed an official agreement of cooperation on June 16, 1951. Although the United States provided the skilled leadership, Ethiopia would pay for the improvement programs. The untimely death of Henry Bennett delayed the program's beginning. Finally on May 16, 1952, an "Agreement Between the Technical Cooperation Administration [Point Four] And Oklahoma Agricultural And Mechanical College" was signed. Under the agreement,

> Oklahoma A. & M. pledged to give assistance to the government of Ethiopia in the establishment and operation of a college of agriculture, a country-wide system of agricultural extension services and agricultural research and experimental stations; to administer other specific projects and operations; and to give assistance to the government in related fields pertaining to the economic developments of Ethiopia.

Oklahoma A & M College president, Oliver S. Wilham, appointed Luther H. Brannon to the Oklahoma A & M contract team to Ethiopia. Brannon was told that "he could fill available positions in Ethiopia with any member of the faculty or administration that he could persuade to go." During the summer of 1952, Brannon worked diligently in the employment, orientation and preparation of the contract personnel. An earlier advance trip had been made to Ethiopia that year by Edward Morrison and Elmo Baumann. These agricultural specialists "surveyed Ethiopia from the air and traveled extensively through the country by four-wheel drive vehicles, carefully noting climate, topography, and plant and animal life." Their notes and collections of soil samples helped the contract team under Brannon to plan the beginning stages of the Ethiopian work.

The original survey contract team, under Brannon's leadership, arrived in Addis Ababa on August 17, 1952. After meeting with Ethiopian officials, the team discussed the project priorities. The first priority was to select a site for the agricultural school. The team then set out to do additional land surveys. They traveled over 5,000 miles the next four months. The school site would have to consider the poor road system, climate and agricultural potential. An earlier agricultural technical school had been built on government-donated land in Jimma, 225 miles southwest of Addis Ababa. The team's first activities were to repair the jungle-infested facilities and bring faculty, along with their families, to begin classes. Massive work was begun to reclaim the buildings and surrounding land. Nearby was the 200-acre Giran farm which the Ethiopian government made available for agricultural research. Eighty students were interviewed, selected and began attending the fall term in 1952. Undependable electricity and water challenged the school community. The team and students overcame many obstacles and hardships to pursue the academic goals before them.

During negotiations with the emperor and the survey team, there was discussion of several possibilities for the permanent site of the agricultural college. By imperial decree, 1,150 acres of land was granted to the school near Harar, 210 miles east of Addis Ababa. The emperor's first visit to the site of the new campus greatly impressed him. He renamed the village and surrounding areas as "Alemaya," which translates "place from which the world may be viewed." The most immediate challenge in beginning construction was the limited number of competent contractors with building experience beyond that of constructing a simple house. The construction bid would not be approved until June 1954.

A dramatic change in philosophy and personnel for the original Point Four program and the contract agreement with Ethiopia was established by the incoming U. S. presidential administration. In 1953, President Dwight D. Eisenhower combined the Technical Cooperation Administration and other technical assistance programs into a new organization called the Foreign Operations Administration (FOA). Harold B. Stassen was named director of the program. A former top administrative official of the Point Four program, and personal friend of Henry Bennett, noted that "most of the key members of the former TCA staff in Washington—a remarkably able and selfless group—have been summarily dismissed." Many of the onsite personnel in Ethiopia were also left causing a loss of valuable, developed relationships of personal trust. The scope of the original projects was expanded to increase the involvement of the FOA in Ethiopian economic and governmental activities. The past, effective direct contact and decision-making connection with Ethiopian locals was now being replaced by more bureaucratic hassle and power plays. The Oklahoma A & M personnel were beginning to develop a problem of low morale with the changes and political interference.

Because of the friendship and contributions of Henry Bennett, Emperor Haile Selassie traveled to Oklahoma to visit the campus of Oklahoma A & M College in Stillwater. The occasion was very special for the campus and the community. On June 18, 1954, the emperor's plane landed at the small Stillwater airport. There was the college band; community, state and national dignitaries; and a large contingent of campus personnel. As the plane door opened and the emperor stood at the top of the steps, the band played the national anthem of Ethiopia. When the anthem ended, the emperor remained standing at the top of the plane's steps. Again the band played the Ethiopian national anthem. Again the emperor remained in place. Someone from the arrival party went up and asked the emperor if he was ready to come down. The emperor said that he would not come down until his country's flag was properly honored. It seemed that someone had mistakenly flown the Ethiopian flag upside down. The mistake was quickly corrected, suitable apologies were made and the planned festivities were able to continue as scheduled. There was a parade through town and the campus.

One of the memorable events of the visit on campus was the emperor's meeting with the family members of Henry Bennett. The emperor told the family how much respect that he had for Dr. Bennett. In Ethiopia, when Dr. Bennett would enter the emperor's throne room, he always obeyed and respected the traditional practice by bowing to the emperor. Upon leaving the room, Dr. Bennett would always back out of the room, showing respect to the emperor by never turning his back to him. The emperor told the family that Dr. Bennett was so respectful of Ethiopian customs that the emperor would return the respect in his visit with the Bennett family. The emperor was not in the habit of shaking hands. Selassie said that he wanted to show his respect for the Bennett family and he would follow the American custom of shaking hands. He formally and respectfully shook hands with each Bennett family member and their invited guests.

The activities at the Alemaya school site were slow and disrupted by inclement weather, newly-replaced Eisenhower administration appointees and the great difficulty of getting parts, supplies and equipment. Another major disruption was the 1956 crisis at the Suez Canal. College students arrived at the Alemaya campus site to help with construction in preparation for the fall semester. The students were graduates and transfers from the Jimma Agricultural Technical School. In November 1956, the college staff and their families were able to move to Alemaya with sewage, water and electrical systems yet to be completed. By the end of 1956, the completed construction projects were "an employees quarters, a power plant building, and installation of an electric generator." By the fall of 1958, four years of instruction had been completed at the Imperial College of Agricultural and Mechanical Arts at Alemaya. The Jimma campus now provided only higher-level education.

After several postponements, the dedication ceremony was held on January 16, 1958. This was an important event for the emperor, the country and the Stillwater college. In the emperor's dedicatory speech, he expressed gratitude to the United States and especially to Dr. Henry G. Bennett, "who laid the plans for the institution and whose great desire and tireless efforts to achieve the establishment of an Agricultural and Mechanical College in this country are well known to us." Following the other official duties, the emperor presented diplomas to eleven students who had completed requirements for graduation. At a reception at the emperor's palace in nearby Dire Dawa, the American advisors were the guests of honor. The re-establishment of the Jimma school and the completion of the Alamaya agricultural college provided a "solid foundation for a nationwide program of agricultural education in Ethiopia." It also modeled the purpose and cooperative spirit foreseen in the Point Four program.

With patience, the Oklahoma A & M personnel began to develop effective lines of cooperation with the new, political administrative leaders and their bureaucratic procedures. The main purpose of the program was to train the Ethiopians "to participate in and eventually carry on the agricultural education program in their country." They were successful in this cause in the 1960s. "From 1957 to 1968 the College of Agriculture graduated 384 students, many of whom received scholarships to continue their education and training in the United States."

Dreams Beyond Point Four

The emperor was recognized as an influential world leader. He helped to organize the Organization of African Unity founded in Addis Ababa in 1963. He frequently traveled around the world building relationships with foreign leaders and powers. Sadly, the final years of the emperor's reign was marked by famine and corruption in the military. As the emperor was growing inarticulate and senile, external political forces were ready to challenge his move toward democratic rule. New obstacles created challenges to the ongoing programs. There was political unrest with the seemingly slow pace of the emperor's promised improved social agendas. There was dissatisfaction with the emperor's new constitution and tax policies. There were several failed attempts of military coups to overthrow the emperor's government. There were natural disasters—floods and droughts—that created unrest. There were even student discipline problems that challenged the college's authority and administrative control. Charges of corruption and economic inflation continued to challenge the emperor's rule. The discontent within the populace and governmental agencies came to a head in January of 1974. The Ethiopian military, with outside Marxist assistance from Cuba, declared a mutiny and began a series of provincial takeovers. By September of that year, the emperor's palace was taken over and nationalized. Selassie was deposed and effectively placed under house arrest. In September of 1975, Emperor Haile Selassie died under questionable circumstances and was secretly buried. In November 2000, his body was finally laid to rest in Addis Ababa's Trinity Cathedral. His opponents have continued to write revisionist history attempting to discredit Selassie's accomplishments and painting him as a dictatorial tyrant with only selfish interests, using oppression and brutality. But the legacy of Haile Selassie is remembered very favorably by those who knew the emperor's heart and his dreams for a better Ethiopia. For many Africans, Selassie "represented the suffering of embattled Africa, torn by colonialism and exploitation." He is often regarded as a symbol of Africa's yearning for freedom. His personal sacrifices and the building of alliances with Henry Bennett, Point Four and the Oklahoma A & M College indicated his strong desire to bring Ethiopia into the twentieth century.

Among the Oklahoma A & M faculty families to settle in Ethiopia were Conrad and Joy Evans. They served in the two Ethiopian schools from 1956 until 1968. They remembered that within the country great respect for the emperor was regional. The struggle between the Point Four program and the USAID was also apparent. The isolation of the American embassy staff diminished the positive aspects of United States foreign policy. The contractual agreement between Ethiopia and Oklahoma A & M College ended in 1968, because the Cubans, then, largely occupied the school at Alameya. The Cuban occupation occurred because the United States withdrew support for the Mengister government and the Russians declared their support. Thus, Cuba, as a Russian ally, was allowed to become active in the local affairs of Ethiopia. The school at Jimma was closed following a student uprising, many of the trained Ethiopian graduates fleeing the country. They would return in the early 1990s as the country began to return to normalcy, reopening the schools. Returning trained leaders would now lead these schools. The Evanses summed up their own work in Ethiopia by valuing "the people that we trained—not bricks and mortar." The effect of those trained leaders continues even today.

The relationship between Emperor Haile Selassie, Henry Bennett, Point Four and the Oklahoma A & M College were of mutual benefit. After Bennett's tragic death in December, 1951, Oklahoma A & M College's new president, Oliver S. Wilham, continued Bennett's dream for international assistance and education. Wilham stated that "history will record Point Four as one of the great historical events in man's development in the world," adding, "I sincerely believe that the work in Ethiopia will go down in history as one of the greatest accomplishments of democracy in the world." The desire of Ethiopian students for education and the willingness of Oklahoma A & M College personnel, such as the Evanses, to endure hardships in Ethiopia serve as a model for dreams and meeting the same needs in the world today.

In the mid 1960s, many events caused a decline in the university's international programs. Following Dr. Bennett's death at the end of 1951, the university relied on Bill Abbott as the link maintaining international outreach activities. With the Ethiopian activities drawing to a close, new university programs were emphasized in Peru and India. But the war in Viet Nam and national unrest caused a distraction from international outreach. The university international outreach organization was also changed. Instead of a centralized international program, each school dean claimed his separate international program. Finally in the early 1990s, the university saw the need to return to a unified international program leadership. Under the leadership of Robert Sandmeyer, a program was developed to provide master's degree-level, academic international studies. With assistance from Oklahoma Congressman Wes Watkins, facilities were provided to house the new international outreach program. In July of 1998, the OSU International Education and Outreach program was approved by the board of regents. The School of International Studies (SIS) was formally dedicated in April of 1999 to fulfill its mission "to provide a university-wide focus to synergize and expand international opportunities in instruction, research and extension for individuals and organizations seeking greater understanding and involvement in world trade and international affairs." In addition to a graduate program, SIS includes the English Language Institute; Study

Abroad/National Student Exchange Office; Peace Corps Recruitment Office; Fulbright Resource Center; OSU Chapter of the Phi Beta Delta International Honor Society; OSU-Mexico Liaison Office and International Outreach Department, which supports statewide, national and international outreach efforts.

Providing the organizational leadership was Dr. James Hromas, the current director. With a committed staff, university funding and cooperation from the school deans, a nationally-respected program of international studies was developed. The program is committed to continue the activities and vision of Dr. Bennett. The Henry G. Bennett Distinguished Fellow awards were created to recognize individuals who have contributed academically to the cause of international studies. In the SIS Center a room has been designated as the "Point Four" room. This room commemorates international ties especially between OSU and Ethiopia. OSU members who have served in Ethiopia and Bennett family members have contributed artifacts and photos which show the success of the special relationship between Bennett and Selaissie. A five hundred year old Ethiopian warrior's shield, a gift from Selaissie to Bennett, is on display. Since the School of International Studies was implemented, 168 students from 16 countries have received master's degrees in international studies with required international experiences. In the spring of 2009, the Oklahoma State University School of International Studies celebrates its tenth anniversary.

The cooperative spirit and common dreams of Haile Selassie and Henry Bennett served as an effective catalyst to achieve the great progress made in Ethiopia. It also served as a model for future effective foreign aid experiences. Although there were setbacks in the original goals, the dreams of both men continue in Ethiopia.

Chapter Six

Benjamin Hardy

A partner in organizing the dreams

Clark Clifford, special counsel to President Truman, stated, "Rarely can an idea be traced back to the mind of one man—especially someone working in the mid-levels of a large bureaucracy—but such was the case with Point Four." That man was Benjamin H. Hardy. Though he sought anonymity in his effort to bring about his personal dreams to help create a better world, only after his untimely death would his behind-the-scenes accomplishments be made known.

Background of a Dreamer

The son of a journalist, Hardy was surrounded all his life by the importance of writing. He was born in Barnesville, Georgia, in 1906. When Hardy was eight years old, his mother died. He was left in the care of his father and two aunts. Having a father who was editor and publisher of a weekly newspaper, he spent many days in his father's newspaper office watching and learning print communication skills. He developed an early love for the business and knew what his career direction would be. Locally educated at a military school, the Gordon Military Institute, Hardy received a top-notch education including his receiving grants and taking college prep school courses. The military training also offered personal benefits for Hardy. He was active as a first captain and won in the competition for the best drill company.

Hardy pursued a career in writing at the University of Georgia. In 1928, he received his bachelor's and master's degrees in journalism, both in a four-year period. In addition to his studies, Hardy was well respected by his peers, elected as president of his class and other school organizations. He was also a Phi Beta Kappa. During the summers he traveled to Europe, thereby learning much about the world and its human needs as well as a wealth of history. He was able to write of these experiences, developing a true worldview.

After graduation Hardy taught first-year English at the University of Georgia for one year. The next year he returned to Barnesville, Georgia, to teach English at his alma mater, the Gordon Military Institute. The following year Hardy became a cub reporter for the *Atlanta Journal*. In 1930, he married a Gordon Military Institute graduate, Christine Moore. She was strongly supportive of his career and shared similar ideals. As a cub reporter, he was assigned the police beat and other low-level duties. He enjoyed the work and experiences even though they focused on the darker side of the human condition.

That same year, Hardy's father being injured in an automobile accident, Hardy left Atlanta to return to Barnesville to run the newspaper for the next two years until his father fully recovered. He made a bold move in 1934, buying the weekly newspaper in Biloxi, Mississippi. He worked hard to make it a daily newspaper. Yet, with the national depression hitting hard and the newspaper losing money, Hardy sold it. In 1935, he joined the Associated Press (AP) in Richmond, Virginia, to work in the state for the next three and a half years. In the fall of 1938, he became a "one-man news bureau" in Roanoke, Virginia, covering the western half of the state for the AP. Benjamin and Christine enjoyed their life and family's growth with the addition of two children.

Several national events would bring Hardy journalistic challenges and recognition. With World War II expanding so was the need for radio news coverage. The AP office in New York inquired among its managers for someone to organize a new office in New York. The AP manager in Richmond said, "We have a man in the western part of the state that can do it." In 1942, they sent Benjamin Hardy and family to New York. While he was effective in his assigned work, he was unhappy with working relationships and the family was unhappy in New York City. He began searching for another job.

When Hardy received a letter asking him to consider working with the State Department in Washington, D.C., he readily accepted the offer. In 1943 the family was delighted to move to the Virginia suburbs. The Inter-American Affairs office sent him to Brazil as press officer in September, 1944. Hardy saw the realities of Brazil and its back-country needs during this two-year period. He observed the life of the Indians, the mining communities and the desert country. These experiences with the Inter-American Affairs work would lay the foundation for Hardy's sense of ways to meet the Brazilian people's needs. When the war concluded, Hardy was offered the job of press officer in the U. S. Embassy in Brazil. In the interest of his family, and especially the children's education, he refused the offer. Another factor in his refusal may have been in the growth of influence and control of the Communists in Brazil.

Making the Dreams Known

Without a job and awaiting return to the United States in April, 1946, Hardy shared with his wife his vision about how to help the people of Brazil and other undeveloped countries. He said that "he had seen enough in Brazil to convince him of what was happening in the world... that the underdeveloped countries *could* be helped tremendously with agricultural, medical, educational facilities to teach them how to do for themselves what needed to be done." It would not be until two years later that Hardy would mention this idea again in response to a question of "how to stop the Russians." That would be significant in the formation of what came to be known as Point Four.

A series of concatenating events would bring Hardy to prominence without pomp. The Hardy family returned from Brazil to their home in Virginia. Hardy was informed by a friend the next day that General Marshall was "looking for him." He went to see General Marshall and immediately accepted the offer of a job as writer for the general and his staff. Hardy truly enjoyed the job and his relationship with General Marshall. Soon afterward, when General Marshall was made secretary of state, Hardy and his staff went with the general. Shortly after, when General Marshall was taken ill and hospitalized, Hardy was transferred to the Public Affairs office in the State Department as a writer and assistant to Francis Russell, director of the Office of Public Affairs.

Another series of events provided the avenue for Hardy's dreams to be expressed. Benjamin Hardy was enjoying his life and his new work. He was delighted with the dramatic victory of Truman over Dewey in November, 1948. On a Sunday morning following the election, the Hardys were to host a big party. Hardy's wife, Christine, made a statement to him, "We really do need to find a way to stop the Russians from taking over the world." Hardy informed her, "I already have the answer, and I have written it in a memorandum to Francis Russell two days ago." That memo would serve as the embryo of the

Point Four program. Russell was very favorable to Hardy's ideas.

After the election of Truman, the White House asked Russell to have someone begin writing the Inaugural Address: Russell asked Hardy. Hardy included his memo in the first draft that was sent to Robert Lovett, who was acting secretary of state in General Marshall's absence. Lovett rejected the concept indicating that the "world was not ready for such an idea as foreign aid in this form..." Lovett asked for a second draft. Hardy's second draft included the same foreign aid idea, Lovett again rejected it and indicated that someone else would write the next draft. It also was unsatisfactory to Lovett. In the first week of December, 1948, Hardy was told to try another draft. This time he made a decision that would put himself and his job in great jeopardy by including his vision within a national, presidential address, but it would prove instrumental in giving birth to the Point Four concept.

Hardy decided to forgo the expected route of sending the draft through Lovett and secretly contacted George Elsey, Truman's White House administrative assistant. They arranged an immediate meeting. When Hardy informed his wife of the danger that he might lose his job doing this, she replied, "Lose it!" Hardy walked across from the State Department to the White House and shared his ideas with Elsey. Elsey was very impressed and knew that Truman would be very receptive to the concept. Benjamin asked Elsey to keep his role in confidence as it would create difficulty for him in the State Department. Elsey contacted Clark Clifford who was working as Truman's White House counsel. Clifford called Francis Russell and cautiously asked for the first draft of the inauguration speech not using Hardy's name. Russell sent over the first draft and Clifford replied "That's what we are looking for." Elsey later recalled, "I was charged with a speech that needed a bright idea and Ben Hardy had a bright idea that was looking for a speech, so the results were obvious." Truman would notify the State Department of his decision to include the fourth point only 48 hours before he gave the speech.

Truman's disappointment in the piecemeal, State Department programs dealing with foreign aid and his repeated failed attempts to get a program more in line with his desires, found that vacuum filled with Hardy's concepts. In his speech, Truman included the following after the first three State Department, approved points:

> Fourth, we must embark on a bold new program for making the
> benefits of our scientific advances and industrial progress available

for the improvement and growth of underdeveloped areas... Our aim should be to help the free peoples of the world, through their own efforts, to produce more food, more clothing, more materials for housing, and more mechanical power to lighten their burdens.

Hardy took great risk in going behind the State Department's leadership. It was because of his dream and sense of rightness of his ideas that he made this decision. With his wife being in complete support and approving of his actions, Hardy felt more confident of his clandestine activities. His desire for anonymity allowed nothing to discredit the concept of Point Four. Although others in the White House certainly worked on the inaugural address, the original words of Benjamin Hardy remained in the speech. Hardy and his wife found it amusing to see, after the speech was given and well received, that others in Washington, D. C. claimed that they were the originators of the Point Four ideas. It was not until after the program was enacted into law and Hardy was selected as the public affairs officer for the Point Four program by Henry Bennett, that Hardy's wife felt she could safely and publicly disclose Hardy's role in the program's creation. She wrote a note to an old friend who was the editor of the *Atlanta Journal* telling him of Hardy's authorship and her disappointment in others trying to take credit for it. Within 48 hours, the head of the Atlanta Journal's Washington Bureau went to see Hardy for confirmation. Hardy, keeping true to his past, would not give him an answer. Only after the reporter questioned with others in the State Department and the White House, did he get confirmation from George Elsey. After the story was published around the southern parts of the nation, Hardy began to receive honors and recognition for his contributions. But inside of Washington, D. C., his role remained uncelebrated.

Years later after Hardy's death, there were still disputes about the program's authorship. But several key players have written confirmation of Hardy's true authorship of the idea. Francis Russell wrote an article in the U. S. Foreign Service Association's *Foreign Service Journal*, April, 1969, attributing authorship of the program to Hardy. George Elsey has given several interviews expressing direct knowledge of Hardy's primary role. Clark Clifford, in his memoirs, *Counsel to the President*, affirms Hardy as the originator of the Point Four program. More than a dozen Truman administration officials also confirm Hardy's significant role. As with the other dreamers, Hardy alone could never have produced the results that his collaboration with the other dreamers was able to accomplish. It is unlikely that Truman alone could have found the voice for his dreams without the collaboration of Benjamin Hardy.

Point Four Dreams

Between the time of the 1949 inaugural speech and the appointment of a program director, the National Education Commission on Educational Policies met in October, 1949. The group's agenda focused on articulating the purpose and direction of the Point Four concepts. By June, 1950, a twenty-seven page document was published entitled "Point Four and Education." The document gave an overview of the international needs, and the suggested direction of the program. Thus, from its genesis, Point Four was conceived of as an educational program that needed an educator as its leader. This report was certainly influential in the selection of a director from the education community, Henry Bennett, for this important program.

Henry Bennett had just been appointed as the director, but Congress and the State Department had changed enough of the original intent from the 1949 inaugural address that Hardy questioned the future of the program. In a personal letter written November 19, 1950, Hardy expressed his concerns about the development of the Point Four program to that date. Hardy stated very candidly

> My greatest concern is that this potentially invaluable asset has not been adequately exploited. The Point Four program which has emerged after much delay falls far short of the great promise that the President's Inaugural pronouncement contained, and which was widely recognized and acclaimed at the time. It may be that with the continued strong support of the President and others who believe in the Point Four concept as devotedly as he does, the effort can gain momentum and yet achieve its purpose. But the election returns appear to me to be ominous for the future of Point Four, despite the merits which in my opinion should appeal to almost all shades of political opinion.

After the inaugural speech had been given, there were strong reactions of approval from all fronts, national and international. The negative reactions came from a few members of Congress and the existing State Department programs that felt threatened and rivalled for foreign aid dollars. At one point in the debates, the Senate came within one vote of killing the program. It took nearly eighteen months before Congress approved the new program officially called the Technical Cooperation Administration (TCA). Henry Bennett's appointment in November, 1951, set the framework for a more independent, educational and a person-to-person rather than just national foreign policy. The challenges and struggles for independent congressional funding were ably met by Henry Bennett. Hardy's concerns for the future of Point Four were being answered by this new Oklahoma director.

Benjamin Hardy became one of Bennett's first selections as he began to assemble his team. Certainly the presidential advisors had made Bennett aware of the contributions that Hardy had made at great risk to his career. Hardy joined the TCA as a public affairs officer, "in order to do what I can to make the program a success." He would make major contributions in helping to develop the organization, communicate its purposes and keep the program true to its original concept. His background in public affairs would provide valuable assistance to Henry Bennett in his speeches and public relations. His relationships within the State Department also provided cautious assistance in keeping Point Four independent while still recognized as a part of the department. He would also develop a deeply personal and respectful relationship with Henry Bennett as a key advisor. Here were two fellow dreamers uniting to try to meet the needs of an impoverished world.

Hardy began immediately to publicize the need for this program. In the early 1950s the Point Four program began to reach out to half of the world's population—over one billion people. Of those masses, eight out of ten were ill-fed, seven out of ten suffered from chronic illnesses, only three out of ten could read and write, the average life expectancy was 41 years of age and half of all infants born in Iran died before their first birthday. The program officially started on October 19, 1950, when the United States and Iran signed a Technical Assistance Agreement, one month before Henry Bennett's appointment as program director was announced.

With Hardy's involvement the Point Four team was developed with adequate funding, and the concept and practice of personal relationships with international leaders and populace was established. Henry Bennett was not satisfied with sitting at a desk in Washington, nor was he satisfied with sitting behind a desk in a foreign country embassy. He wanted direct, personal contact with leaders and the common people. He traveled to the fields to see the needs and the progress of the program's efforts. He often took key leaders with him on these trips. Hardy would travel with him and be able to communicate the program's significance to the press, foreign leaders and congressional leadership back home.

Although no one trumpeted the leadership of Hardy, the fact of the matter is that he was one of the hands-on team leaders. The team traveled to Central and South America January-February, 1951. This was one of the rare occasions when Mrs. Bennett traveled with her husband. Benjamin Hardy had the highest respect and admiration for Mrs. Bennett as a valued team member. He was amazed and amused at how she supported Dr. Bennett in his work. Fortunately, she kept a detailed daily diary of the trip from her perspective. Although she did not participate in all of the high-level, personal meetings with the TCA team and national leaders, she did give her candid impressions of the populace within each country. She attested to the growing negative influence of communism as it began to gain control in several South American countries. She observed the progressive impact that Point Four was having with the people where program assistants were allowed to train and implement the technical improvement in agriculture and education. She also bore witness to the very positive impact the program was having in promoting a growing respect for the United States with the fulfillment of Hardy's and Bennett's dreams.

As Benjamin Hardy had been behind the scenes writing many of the speeches for James Webb and others in the State Department and assisting in the key part of Truman's 1949 inaugural address, now he was actively behind the scenes writing speeches and articles for Henry Bennett and the Point Four program. It is safe to assume that his speech writing for Point Four was more personal, having an even higher motivation than in his past work. Seeing his dreams coming together with the dreams of Truman and Bennett, he expressed his dreams in a 1950 letter to a personal friend in North Carolina,

> While I do not intend to seek any personal advantage from my part in the genesis of Point Four, I am proud of the contribution I was able to make, not only in formulating the Point Four concept, but also in framing and drafting much of the language used in the inaugural address, which I think admirably served the purpose for which it was intended and, potentially at least, did have the impact of a 'democratic manifesto.'

Bennett and Hardy made many other trips during 1951. Among those were trips to Europe. During a visit to Rome, Henry Bennett took time to write a very personal letter to his daughter, Liberty. On July 5, 1951, he wrote of a very significant site visit:

> I've visited the underground caves just outside of Rome called the Catacombs where early Christians were buried and where they held their worship while being persecuted. You walk thru these long underground tunnels and the only light you have is from a little candle they give you. This is to make it appear just like it did to those early Christians.

The experience was very meaningful to Bennett because of his strong, Christian faith. It was also symbolic of what Dr. Bennett and the Point Four team were trying to do—to light a small candle in countries and lives darkened by the ravages of war. Little is known of Hardy's religious commitments and he was not as openly expressive to others about his faith as Bennett.

In November, 1951, Hardy, Bennett and the Point Four team prepared for an ambitious trip around the world with a scheduled return for January, 1952. Mrs. Bennett would again accompany the team along with A. Cyril Crilley (foreign affairs officer) and James T. Mitchell (audio visual materials officer). Mitchell would serve as the trip public relations person recording the trip activities with photos and on film. Dr. Bennett was initially invited to speak at the sixth annual meeting of the Food and Agriculture Organization in Rome, Italy, on December 4, 1951. While in Rome, Dr. Bennett was invited to speak on CBS radio. Hardy was certainly involved in preparing Bennett's remarks. An aide said that "Henry knocked them over; he really went to town, with a simple direct message on what Point IV hoped to accomplish."

Hardy and Bennett incorporated additional visits to key Point Four programs around the world during the trip to Rome. There were scheduled plans after Rome to visit Athens, Greece; Cairo, Egypt; Amman, Jordan; Beirut, Lebanon; Damascus, Syria; Baghdad, Iraq; Teheran, Iran; Karachi, Pakistan; Dehli, Bombay, Colombo, Madras and Calcutta, India; Ceylon; Bangkok, Thailand; Hong Kong; and Tokyo, Japan. James Mitchell recorded the first half of the trip in photos and a wonderful brief film. There were numerous scenes of Rome with the Point Four team members pictured. The air flight to Greece and Egypt was recorded with scenes of the Parthenon and the Pyramids. An interesting scene was also recorded of the farmers in the Egyptian fields using steel points on their plows. These steel points, replacing the inefficient wooden points, had been provided by Point Four. Also recorded were scenes from Jordan, Israel, Lebanon and Iraq. Just before the team boarded the Egyptian airline for the fateful trip to Iran, Mitchell mailed the photos and film back to the State Department.

Tragic Death and Legacy of the Dreams

The key leaders of the Point Four program were lost in the terrible airplane crash in the Iranian mountains just north of the Teheran airport. With the specific losses of Henry Bennett and Benjamin Hardy, the Point Four program would never again have the public relations impact it had in its first year. December 23, 1951, one day after the crash, the U. S. State Department issued a statement concerning Hardy's life:

> Benjamin H. Hardy was one of the first and strongest enthusiasts for the Point 4 idea. An able public affairs officer in the Department of State, and a remarkably eloquent writer, he helped to create, explain and interpret the idea of technical cooperation. In his modest and self-effacing way, he consistently refused to take credit for his part in bringing Point 4 to life in the minds of his colleagues in the Department and in interpreting its purposes to the public.

On December 24, 1951, the *Atlanta Journal* gave the following tribute:

> But what could be more in the spirit of The One whose birth we celebrate this week than the self-sacrificing, self-effacing service of Ben Hardy, who was consumed with the ambition to carry out his great plan but totally lacked the ambition to seek any credit for himself.

Like the other fellow dreamers, Hardy left a lasting legacy in his family. For example, his son, Ben Hardy, III, was thirteen years old when his father died. In 1959, he received a bachelor's degree with honors in foreign affairs from the University of Virginia; a master's degree in international relations from George Washington University in

1965; and a Ph.D. in political science from the University of Chicago in 1977. During these years he also completed military duty in the Army Reserves and worked as a foreign service officer in the U. S. Department of State, serving in Germany and Mali. He then actively pursued consulting and professional assignments. He specialized as a consultant on African economic and political development. As his father, Ben Hardy performed generously in the public sphere because of a supportive family. Married to Caroline, they raised four children together and currently reside in Connecticut.

Following Benjamin Hardy's tragic death, his widow, Christine, remarried and continued to keep the Benjamin Hardy Point Four connections known. In an oral interview given in 1973, she predicted that "within 75 years there's going to be, well, I called it a …rebirth in the entire world through this Point 4 concept. It's bound to come. How it will be called, who will do it, who the President will be, but it's going to unfold. I call it a fine idea."

The great historian, Arnold Toynbee predicted that President Truman's call for wealthy nations to come to the aid of the world's poor "will be remembered as the signal achievement of the age." On January 20, 1999, a special Point Four 50th Anniversary Commemoration paid remembrance to Hardy and fellow dreamers in the State Department in Washington, DC. Among the special guests were Benjamin Hardy, Jr. and George Elsey. An unveiled plaque honored President Truman; Benjamin H. Hardy, Jr.; Clark M. Clifford; Francis Russell and Henry G. Bennett. The USAID Administrator's Conference Room was officially named the "Point Four Room." Yet, the type of remembrance needed is not only commemorative, but also emulative. When compared to foreign aid national programs that followed, Point Four stands as the high mark, even today, for international respect and accomplishment. The joining together of fellow dreamers—Bennett, Truman and Hardy— with common goals and common ideals, would bring the possibility of hope for the dreams of needy families around the world.

Chapter Seven

James E. Webb

A national team player in realizing the dreams

Another individual who had an important interrelationship with Henry Bennett was James Edwin Webb. Unlike the life-long relationship Bennett had with Holloway or the career-long collaborations Bennett shared with Kerr, the relationship between Webb and Bennett was comparatively short-term. Although Webb's relationship with Henry Bennett began late in both of their lives, it continued with Bennett's family long after Bennett's death.

Background of a Dreamer

Coming from a part of the country that was more reflective of the deep South, James Edwin Webb was born into a family of educators and dreamers. His father, John Frederick Webb was superintendent of schools for twenty-six years in Granville County, North Carolina. Webb was born on October 7, 1906 to John and Sarah Gorham Webb at Tally Ho, North Carolina. His early education was in North Carolina schools at an impressionable time during World War I. His family not being wealthy, as a young man, he assisted with the family income by working at typical, small-town jobs: farm work, newspaper delivery, magazine sales, dime store clerking and driving a truck on construction sites. During this period, he learned important values from his father and mother, such as his father's idealism and his mother pragmatism. He went to the University of North Carolina where his studies were delayed until he could earn money from a job offered to him by local businessman, R. G. Lassiter. Receiving his bachelor of arts degree in 1928, he was remembered by his classmates as having a "photographic memory" and active in a variety of campus activities. Upon graduation, during the time of the Great Depression, he enlisted in the Marine Corps and became a second lieutenant. He entered the newly-formed aviation school and competed with others who were in the upper class and had come from ivy-league schools. He reflected later that "that was the first place, I think, that I realized I could compete with the wealthy fellows from Harvard and Princeton and so forth…I started at the very bottom, just getting by." He was commissioned as a second lieutenant and assigned to the East Coast Expeditionary Force at Quantico, Virginia, serving as a pilot on active duty from 1930–1932. Webb's employment, education and military experiences served him well for the national and international duties he world be called upon to do in the years ahead. He would find the political experience and contacts invaluable in the next phase of his career.

After military duty Webb became secretary to Congressman Edward W. Pou, 4th North Carolina District, who was then chairman of the powerful House Rules Committee, yet he himself was elderly and sickly. Pou's congressional office needing organization and management, Webb provided that service, accompanying Pou to congressional meetings and briefings with prominent congressional leaders. President Roosevelt's "New Deal" programs were enthusiastically supported by Webb as reflections of his father's idealistic and his mother's practical philosophies. In 1934, Webb assisted in the Washington, D. C. office of O. Max Gardner, an attorney and former governor of North Carolina. That same year, as a condition of his new employment, he enrolled at George Washington University to study law. In 1936 he was admitted to the bar of the District of Columbia. During this time Webb was influential in helping settle a national dispute with the Army Air Corps over airmail contracts. As a result of his involvement with the dispute, Webb was invited to consider working for the Sperry Gyroscope Company. In the spring of 1936, he became personnel director, secretary-treasurer and later vice president of the Sperry Gyroscope Company in Brooklyn, New York. The workforce had expanded from eight hundred to thirty thousand people with the growing demands of World War II. Just as Webb found his business career growing, he also felt the need to grow in his personal life. In 1938 he married Patsy Aiken Douglas. Patsy was a very positive help to him. Her social skills and intelligence served them both well as he rose in the company ranks. In 1944 Webb reentered the Marine Corps for active duty in World War II. Another motivation to bolster the war effort came when Webb's brother, Gorham, became a prisoner of war at a Japanese POW camp. After World War II Webb returned home, again serving as assistant to O. Max Gardner, who had become undersecretary of the Treasury and would become director of the Bureau of Budget in the executive office of the president. He and Patsy had two children: Sarah Gorham Webb, born February 27, 1945, and James Edwin Webb, Jr., born March 5, 1947.

Supporting National Dreams

From such rigorous training and work experience, Webb offered a keen analytical and useful approach to one of President Truman's most pressing problems: Webb was asked by Truman to reduce the war budget. The challenges facing the office of the Bureau of Budget were tremendous. Under Roosevelt the office held little significance. Truman saw the need for better cooperation and communication with the national budget process. The national economy was shifting from wartime to peacetime. Despite Webb's telling Truman that he was not very interested in the job as director of the Bureau of Budget, Truman persisted. When the president went to announce Webb's new position to the press, Truman could not remember Webb's name and promised to get back to the press. Despite the initial faux pas, Webb eventually developed a close and trusting relationship with the president. Truman once told Webb, "You know, I understand facts and figures and I regard the economic picture as the very lifeblood of our country and our government. You and I must work this out together, and I will work with you." And they did work together closely. They met regularly in well-planned, fifteen-minute meetings, during which there was a mutual exchange of information. With Webb's encouragement, Truman's 1947 State of the Union address included, for the first time, the president's budget message.

Webb held a great responsibility with the Bureau of the Budget. All departments, cabinet members and legislative programs had to submit operational costs and income to the director. The director then educated the president on the programs and in turn reflected the president's views to the submitters. This was often a source of conflict with power-hungry individuals within and without the administration. There were even times when Webb disagreed with a Truman proposal and he was permitted to express his views before a cabinet meeting.

Webb, having special knowledge and preparation at such occasions, usually found the president's final decision to favor his own. His purpose was never selfish, but always looking out for the president's and the nation's best interests.

Webb was presented with new and shifting budget responsibilities. In 1947, President Truman reorganized all of the military branches under Secretary of Defense, James V. Forrestal, who demanded increased budget spending. The creation of the Marshall Plan required significant budget expenditures to aid worn-torn Europe from falling under Soviet influence. The plight of returning soldiers and their needs also affected the federal budget. The State Department was requesting a sizeable increase in funds to combat Soviet aggression. All of these new directions tested Webb's oversight responsibilities and skills in diplomacy.

Webb also served as the liaison between former President Herbert Hoover and President Truman during the two years of the Hoover Commission. The commission was to study and recommend a more efficient reorganization of the federal government. Since these decisions involved budget and legislative approval, Webb's participation was vital to its success.

Webb effectively used the political and communication skills gained from his past Washington experiences. He began to meet regularly with legislators to educate them on particular budget concerns. He involved key congressional leaders, crossing party lines, in promoting needed budget programs. Hence, the Marshall Plan funding approval was made less contentious because of Webb's personal communication. Unavoidably, however, the budget battles in Washington were worsened by the approaching 1948 national election. Many believed in the inevitability of a Republican victory. Some department heads, such as Secretary of Defense Forrestal, even began to secretly contact the Republican presidential candidate, Thomas Dewey, with inside information. Forrestal's hope was that his department leadership would continue under Dewey. Webb played a major role in keeping Truman informed of such activities and maintaining Truman's national budget on target to continue operations in a second administration.

After Truman's re-election, Webb considered leaving government service and accepting an offer to be the dean of the school of commerce at the University of North Carolina, which could possibly be a pathway to the university's presidency. However, Truman's White

House counsel, Clark Clifford, had a direct offer from the president. Clifford told Webb that Secretary of State George C. Marshall, and his undersecretary, Robert A. Lovett, were leaving the administration. He then told Webb that Truman was going to appoint Dean Acheson as secretary of state and wanted Webb to be his undersecretary. When Webb questioned his own ability in the area of foreign policy, Clifford told him that "a certain amount of [bureaucratic] orderliness is necessary in foreign relations, and the President feels that you could provide that and provide it in a way that he would feel very happy with." Webb was also reassured that Acheson had approved of him in that position. Webb's great admiration for Truman and his sense of public duty led him to accept the position. Webb was appointed undersecretary of state on January 7, 1949.

Just as with the other fellow dreamers, Webb's rise in national service was not an isolated act. He was dependent on others to help him in his accomplishments. In 1949, Webb's life made a dramatic change as he was asked by President Truman to serve as undersecretary of state of the U. S. State Department, serving under Secretary Dean Acheson. Acheson "handled the substantive foreign policy, while Webb handled the department's administration and supervised the reorganization of the department as recommended by the Hoover Commission." It was also at this time that President Truman had introduced his Point Four program in his 1949 inaugural address. Point Four was not favored by many leaders in the State Department. Interagency fighting for funding and control of foreign aid was distracting from the genuine needs of the world after the devastation of World War II. In his modest demeanor, Webb kept peace within the State Department. His experience with the national budget, his awareness of Truman's objectives as president and Webb's familiarity with Washington D. C. outsiders such as Henry Bennett, all helped Webb to bring a more cooperative cohesion within the executive branch of government at a critical time. The rise of communistic influence and dominance in many war-torn countries was a threat to democratic growth. Webb would be a key link between the State Department and President Truman. He would also be an important link between the State Department directorship transition of George Marshall and Dean Acheson. Webb was the perfect complement to Acheson in the State Department which was then known to be unmanageable. While Acheson's self-confidence to the point of arrogance would offend many, Webb's quiet, behind-the-scenes personal contacts would soften Acheson's brusqueness. With Acheson's inability to effectively organize and oversee a mass bureaucracy, Webb offered the background skills and positive personal attributes to accomplish the tasks. Webb's experiences in the Bureau of Budget office also made him aware that in the annual budget battles, the State Department was losing ground to the Defense Department. Acheson told Webb to act immediately in the State Department's reorganization, knowing of the disruptions and dissatisfactions of top leadership. Webb related to congressional leaders, enabling him to secure legislative approval for the reorganization plans. The reorganization plans allowed for a stronger secretary of state, pleasing Acheson. Having a stronger secretary of state also pleased President Truman. However, a stronger secretary of state did not please the competing secretary of defense.

Secretary of Defense Louis Johnson was a formidable figure in Washington with great political influence and powerful contacts. At every chance he used his influence and contacts to discredit Acheson. He was greatly aided by the growing hysteria of anti-communism created by the House Un-American Activities Committee. As Acheson appeared before a congressional committee hearing, his sarcasm and scorn at the process brought him more enemies and ill will. Again, it was Webb who would try to mend fences with personal meetings concerning erroneous accusations and Secretary Johnson's constant sniping.

Since Webb entered State Department service in January, 1949, it is uncertain how much knowledge or involvement he had with what was to become the Point Four program. His role as budget director certainly brought him into discussions of where Truman wanted to go with foreign aid spending. He was certainly aware of Truman's mistrust and disappointment in the State Department's ability to catch his vision for a positive foreign aid program. He may not have been aware in his early role as undersecretary of the back channels used by Benjamin Hardy to introduce the Point Four concept in the White House. As Truman's 1949 inaugural address was being written, it is uncertain how much direct knowledge or input that Webb may have had in the secret inclusion of Point Four. It is also uncertain how much knowledge or influence Webb would have had in the selection of Dr. Henry Bennett as the director of the Point Four program. But it is certain that Webb was Truman's man in the State Department. Hardy, in his capacity as speech writer for the state department, prepared a number of

Webb's speeches. In one of those speeches prepared by Hardy, Webb spoke at the University of North Carolina, in June, 1949, stating,

> One of the greatest changes that has occurred in this period is that you and I are no longer citizens of a nation that is merely one among many. We are citizens of the nation to which free people of the world look for leadership and security. This turn of history places on the United States a tremendous responsibility, which all of its citizens share and will continue to share for many years.

Webb would be tested once again in June, 1950, at the outbreak of North Korean aggression. Webb was one of the three advisors who met with Truman immediately after North Korea had invaded South Korea. They worked to temper Truman's desire to retaliate immediately with overwhelming, unilateral, military might. Webb, along with Dean Rusk, Dean Acheson and Louis Johnson, presented the president with three positions of response. Acheson was undergoing severe attacks in the press over his supposed softness on communism, and he had to be careful of his role in the presidential decision to take action. It was Webb who presented the three positions to Truman and helped him to arrive at a well-thought-out response. The result was agreement to work through the United Nations with a unified international response.

Webb's continuing role as official and unofficial liaison between the State Department and the Oval Office is known. Bennett family contacts indicate that it was James Webb who personally called Henry Bennett to offer him the job as director of what would officially become the Point Four program. Thus, at some key level, Webb was the liaison between Bennett and Truman in reporting and evaluating the Point Four program's impact. As Point Four was Truman's pet project and Bennett was Truman's handpicked director, Webb would have had a close connection with the program's operations.

Webb was deeply affected by the tragic deaths of Bennett and Hardy. As a colleague and friend, he prepared official remarks from the State Department in response to their deaths. It is ironic that the man for whom Hardy had written so many speeches, would now write in regard to the loss of Hardy. In tribute to Henry Bennett, Webb would write on January 7, 1952,

> His strength came from her [Oklahoma's] soil. His vision was as wide as her horizons. From the history of her early days and from

his own youth grew his unshakable belief in the dignity of work. In particular, he valued the man who worked the land.

I know these things because in the past year we worked together in a close day-to-day relationship. I watched Point Four grow under his guidance. At the time of his death, it was beginning to bear fruit in many lands. I am convinced that this growth was possible because Dr. Bennett was driven by a single passion—he loved his fellow man. That love was wise, understanding, and above all practical.

Webb faced numerous personal, national and international challenges that negatively affected his ability to continue successful State Department leadership. The stress of McCarthyism, the loss of public servants such as Bennett and Hardy and the frustrations of the Korean Conflict caused Webb to consider his status in government service after the Truman administration. He continued interest in political affairs serving as an informal foreign policy adviser to Senator Robert S. Kerr who "was making an unsuccessful campaign for the 1952 Democratic presidential nomination." There continued to remain that element of mutual support among meaningful friends and dreamers.

Leading National Dreams

With the end of the Truman administration in early 1953, James Webb left Washington, D. C. to relocate in Oklahoma City, Oklahoma. He became a director and assistant to the president of Kerr-McGee Oil Industries. Webb also served as president of the Republic Supply Company, a subsidiary of the Kerr-McGee Oil Corporation. This was at a time when the Oklahoma City oil basin was booming and fortunes were being made. However, James Webb was not content to simply remain in Oklahoma and pursue personal business interests. He still maintained strong visions for his community and country. In 1954, the Oklahoma City Chamber of Commerce organized the Frontiers of Science Committee under the leadership of Dean A. McGee, president of Kerr-McGee Oil Industries. The purpose was to develop strategies to relate education, research and industrial development in the region and state. Also motivating the efforts were the threats of Russia's scientific advancements. In the early fall of 1955, "the Oklahoma City Chamber of Commerce Committee, which had acted as a nucleus, stepped aside and men from all parts of the state formed the Frontiers of Science Foundation, Inc." The officers of the foundation were as follows: Chairman of the Board Dean A. McGee; Vice Chairman of the Board E. K. Gaylord; Executive Director Dr. Robert MacVicar (dean of the Graduate School at Oklahoma A & M College); and President James E. Webb. Another important dreamer was Richard W. Poole, an economics educator, who served as assistant to Webb. These dreamers saw the need and the advantage of scientific advancement. The foundation's work was funded by private contributions and commitments of $400,000. The three main goals were "science information, science education and science installation." An immediate result was seen in the increase of enrollment in Oklahoma higher education math and science classes by nearly 125%. President Dwight D. Eisenhower wrote the following concerning the program in a letter to Governor Raymond Gary:

> I have observed with appreciation the splendid work of the recently established Frontiers of Science Foundation of Oklahoma, created and financed by your own people through popular subscription, in order to upgrade and encourage science teaching in your public schools and institutions of higher learning; to provide better opportunity for young people; and to help meet the great need for more and better trained scientists and engineers.

In April, 1956, Webb announced the hiring of Phil Bennett, Henry Bennett's son, as vice president and secretary of the Republic Supply Company. Phil would also play an active role in the Frontiers of Science Foundation activities. These two lives would now become very entwined with business and future science technology.

Events in the Russian space program caused immediate reactions throughout the United States regarding scientific and military concerns. On October 4, 1957, the Russians orbited Sputnik I, the world's first artificial satellite. One month later Sputnik II was also successfully launched with a dog as passenger. The United States Congress authorized creation of the National Space and Aeronautics Administration including funding and personnel. Several launch failures led to more national concern, especially with a Cold War atmosphere.

James Webb's career benefited from his relationship with Senator Kerr in 1960. When Lyndon Johnson was elected vice president, Kerr replaced him as chairman of the Senate Aeronautical and Space

Science Committee. Kerr recommended Webb's appointment as the new head of the National Aeronautics and Space Administration (NASA). The very early Project Mercury one-man flight activities of NASA were led by the first director, T. Keith Glennan. Webb followed him, only after "being personally requested by President Kennedy." The position was seen as unimportant as it had been turned down by at least 18 or 19 other persons. Webb was well prepared for the position and its challenges with his experiences in public and private life. Described as being "Washington-wise," Webb had acquired "understanding of the environments, problems, capabilities, and limitations of the federal government, private industry, and educational institutions." Webb easily sailed through the senate confirmation hearings. Then on February 14, 1961, Webb was sworn in by Vice President Johnson at NASA's temporary home in the Dolly Madison House on Lafayette Square.

Events that followed caused a major shift in priorities and importance for NASA and James Webb. Another Russian achievement increased national concern. On April 12, 1961, Soviet cosmonaut Yuri Gagarin orbited the earth becoming the first man in space. Webb had now convinced President Kennedy, with Vice President Johnson's influence, that the space program should be broadened far beyond that of a lunar landing and return. President Kennedy recommended a program that was aimed at "advancing space research and development on a broad front with a new family of large boosters, communications and meteorological satellites, scientific satellites, and exploration of the planets." These programs would set the objectives for NASA for the next eight to ten years.

Under Webb's leadership, NASA was encouraged by the successful, first Mercury space flight carrying Alan Shepherd on May 5, 1961. Pressure was building to beat the Soviets at some level in the space race. In daily meetings with the vice president, Webb maintained the balance between the political pressure and technological capabilities. He told Johnson with assurance that a lunar landing was "the first project we could assure the president that we could do and do ahead of the Russians…" Webb further indicated that "there's got to be political support over a long period of time, like ten years…" Before Johnson approached the president with this information, he consulted with his friend and Senator from Oklahoma, Robert Kerr. Kerr told Johnson that "if Jim Webb says we can land a man on the moon and bring him back safely home, then it can be done."

President Kennedy delivered a major speech to the Congress on May 25, 1961, in which he announced that the "United Sates would embark on a policy designed to send a man to the moon by the end of the decade." The immediate result was an "increase of NASA's annual budget from $1 billion to more than $5 billion dollars during the mid-1960s." Webb led the agency in making major decisions directly affecting cities and states. He "chose Cape Kennedy as the launching site; he led the development of the two-man Gemini project to lead to the three-man Apollo moon shots; and he selected the technology and contractors for the booster rockets, command modules, and earth station equipment." His relationship with the Kennedy administration reflected his unwavering devotion to control operations. When someone in the White House suggested to him a good location for a NASA procurement, "Webb replied with a blistering memo to Ken O'Donnell—which was intended for Kennedy's eyes—which simply said, 'You run the White House, I'll run NASA.'" That was the attitude which Webb conveyed to the Bureau of the Budget and the Congress.

Webb dealt with organizational and "turf" issues as effectively for NASA as he did at the State Department. At the State Department Webb sought to establish sole authority for foreign policy from competitors such as the Department of Defense. He fought similar battles to establish NASA as the sole authority for space policy from the familiar Department of Defense competition. The Air Force sought to maintain control of the development of the essential booster rocket program. Webb was able to win this battle for NASA enlisting the support of Defense Department director, Robert McNamara. When the Apollo program was outlined in a memo coming from Webb and McNamara, President Kennedy approved the program exactly as it was laid out. Webb's personal agenda for NASA was also solidified. He saw a program to establish "a mission to use science and technology, and now Apollo, to strengthen the United States educationally and economically, the Oklahoma Frontiers of Science effort writ large."

Webb continued to benefit from his past relationship with Senator Kerr. Kerr had told Johnson of Webb's independent experiences at Kerr-McGee in Oklahoma. Kerr successfully advised Johnson to let Webb "do his business and not try to control him." Kerr was by far the most influential man in the Senate and he was Webb's greatest supporter. He maneuvered political approval for NASA programs and defended the program from political and business competitors. Webb returned the favors by accompanying Kerr back home to Oklahoma where he held meetings on space policy, always careful to emphasize Kerr's major role in this dramatic and vital success.

Webb continued to fight the battles for NASA supremacy and authority in the space program. These battles were fought internally as well as externally. Internally, there were challenges from some leadership within NASA who sought to rise to more independent control in their assigned areas. Some among the leadership had difficulty operating in consultations and with economic and political priorities. Externally, Webb continued to wrestle for exclusive NASA control of all space flights. Defense Director McNamara tried unsuccessfully to secure Defense Department oversight of all earth orbit flights leaving NASA only with control of space flight. President Kennedy unsuccessfully explored the possible cooperative venture with the Soviet Union on space flights. Webb's success in keeping NASA in control was dealt a significant blow with the sudden death of Senator Robert Kerr in January of 1963. The new chairman of the Senate Space Committee was Clinton P. Anderson, from New Mexico. He and Webb had had differences while Webb served as budget director under Truman. Anderson carried those differences with him into the overseeing of the space program under Webb's leadership. The battles were increasingly harder to win for Webb and NASA.

The tragic assassination of President John F. Kennedy on November 22, 1963, shocked the nation and the world. With President Johnson vowing to continue the programs in place, Webb and NASA had a strong ally who understood and supported their efforts and direction. NASA continued to grow in its outreach and incorporation of educational, industrial and scientific facilities and personnel. Because of the growing military obligations to Viet Nam and Johnson's New Society programs, NASA's expenditures and requests were being watched and challenged.

During this time period, Webb kept a very low profile. He even stayed in Washington, D. C. during all launches "to implement damage control in the event of any mishap." Sadly, his services would be needed to provide damage control for a serious accident in the Apollo program. On January 27, 1967, the Apollo-Saturn (AS) 204 was on the launch pad at the Kennedy Space Center, Florida, going through simulation tests. A flash fire killed the three astronauts aboard—"Gus" Grissom, Edward White and Roger Chaffee. A shocked nation and Congress waited for answers and explanations. Webb went personally to President Johnson and asked that NASA be allowed to investigate the accident and direct the Apollo program's recovery. In an honest investigation, Webb personally sought "to discover the details of the tragedy, to correct problems, and to get back on schedule." Webb reported the accident findings to numerous congressional committees and took a severe beating with each committee. The effect was personal humiliation for Webb, but he deflected blame from NASA and the Johnson administration. Webb took direct actions to prevent such a tragedy from happening again. He negotiated with contractors on improved designs and materials. He encouraged the astronauts-in-training to speak candidly with NASA leadership and honestly answer congressional investigative committee questions. He worked hard to defend NASA even from the attacks by Senator Anderson of the Senate Space Committee. There were charges of covering up some of the investigative findings and of cronyism in hirings related back to Kerr's involvement. Webb worked hard to regain NASA's credibility and organizational effectiveness.

The successful launch of Apollo 4 on November 9, 1968, was a great psychological and political boost for NASA. However, the strain on NASA leadership was beginning to show. Several top leaders within the organization resigned in order to return to their academic and scientific communities. Funding from Congress was becoming increasingly difficult to achieve, especially as national elections were underway. Webb was able to replace NASA leadership with very capable personnel. He also began to think about his own position with NASA and its future. He saw himself as the lightning rod for NASA critics and thought about his replacement. He began to groom his very capable assistant, Thomas Paine.

Webb approached an over-occupied President Johnson about his possible resignation from NASA. Johnson discussed the possibility of a cabinet position. Webb declined knowing that there would be substantial political turnover after an election. President Johnson then told Webb that he would not seek reelection as president. Webb would be one of very few who knew before it was announced. Webb told Johnson, "Mr. President, the day you leave the White House is the day I will leave NASA." In typical Johnson fashion, he indicated that he wanted to announce it immediately, even before Webb talked to his wife, Thomas Paine or the NASA organization. As word spread, there was much speculation about the decision and the president's quick announcement. But on October 7, 1968, Jim Webb's birthday, he left NASA, just months before the Apollo program's successful moon landing in July, 1969. At that time, over 400,000 individuals were involved in NASA programs. Only 35,000 of these were actual NASA employees. Others were involved with "the Department of Defense, industry, universities, and other private sector institutions." Over 20,000 companies were involved.

The country's response to his resignation was mixed. However, the national media had a more objective reaction. A *Wall Street Journal* article on October 11, 1968 reacted to Webb's sudden resignation. In part the article stated:

> A good deal of this criticism may be unfair and exaggerated, and most of it misses the point. Mr. Webb probably deserves far more credit than he will ever receive for his achievements with the space program. Beneath the bluster, NASA's administrator was smart, honest and independent. Most of all, he had the courage to confront the conflicts—with astronauts, associates, contractors and Congress—which threatened to undermine the agency. "He had guts and imagination," concedes one non-admirer.

Webb's role in NASA was not forgotten. Apollo 7 was launched on October 11, this time with a proud former NASA director in attendance. The three Apollo 7 astronauts and Webb were awarded NASA's highest honor, the Exceptional Service Medal, presented by President Johnson. When Johnson presented the award to Webb, he departed from his written presentation notes and commented to him, "Jim Webb, you are the best." A month later President Johnson presented Jim Webb with the Presidential Medal of Freedom, the highest honor a president can bestow on any individual. President Kennedy's and Webb's goal had been achieved. President Nixon was advised to keep Thomas Paine in NASA leadership to ensure the successful lunar landing on July 20, 1969, completing Webb's careful preparations.

Much study has been done of Webb's leadership style and practices during this challenging time for the United States. He role was described as "where the right man and the right times came together effectively." Webb's NASA leadership has been described with six distinct elements: understanding and mastery of the total job; building an effective management team; maintaining flexibility required to cope with challenging environmental factors; building and integrating processes against centrifugal forces; focusing on the critical elements of the job and developing and continually adjusting feedback systems.

"He steps down, so he insists, to devote his time to helping younger men advance their careers," wrote an objective observer about Webb. He did continue to advise and lecture wherever he could. He certainly did spend generous amounts of time helping young men grow in their career experiences. One of those was Dr. Richard Poole who remembers his experiences with James Webb as a great and stern mentor. He recalls Webb's kindnesses and valuable lessons in administration and public service. Dr. Poole achieved great recognition as a professor and executive vice president of Oklahoma State University.

In 1969 Webb wrote a book, *Space Age Management: The Large-Scale Approach.* The book was based on a series of lectures given at Columbia University toward the end of his time at NASA. Regrettably, Webb did not write a memoir of his experiences in government and public service. But after NASA, his national public service was not completed. In 1970, Webb was approved by Congress to be a citizen regent of the board of regents of the Smithsonian Institution. He had been recruited to this position by Chief Justice of the Supreme Court, Warren E. Burger, who had been appointed by President Nixon. Until 1982, Webb served in outstanding administrative leadership as head of the executive committee. He employed his experiences in administration and his close Washington contacts to increase funding threefold, expanding the operations and facilities of the Smithsonian. Burger observed that Webb "served with loyalty and commitment, and helped assure an effective decision-making process and a spectacular set of achievements."

Sadly, in 1975, at age sixty-nine, Webb was diagnosed with Parkinson's disease. The disease affects the nervous system and eventually leaves the patient totally dependent on others. Webb challenged the disease head-on with daily regimens hoping to delay the effects as long as possible. Limiting his daily work schedule and establishing a vigorous exercise program helped to put off the debilitating effects. In September 1981, Webb traveled to West Point where he received the Sylvanus Thayer Award to "honor distinguished Americans whose service and accomplishments in the national interest exemplified devotion to the ideals expressed in the U. S. Military Academy's motto 'Duty, honor, country.'"

After resigning from the Smithsonian Board of Regents in 1982, Webb began to slow down his ventures away from the loving home provided by his faithful wife, Patsy. As he began to feel the debilitating effects of Parkinson's disease, he provided challenges to his family and close friends. Finally, on March 27, 1992, at age eighty-five, James Webb died of a heart attack. He was buried with high honors at Arlington National Cemetery. President George Bush, expressing sympathy to Webb's widow, Patsy, expressed these words concerning James Webb:

> He will always be remembered as the man who guided the newly created space agency to its extraordinary success in the 1960s, culminating in the historic walk on the Moon by an American astronaut. That single event is among this country's proudest moments. It represents one of the greatest scientific, engineering, and managerial accomplishments of the 20th century, and its success is a great tribute to Jim's leadership at NASA. The American people will always be grateful for his lasting contribution to our nation and, indeed, to the entire world."

Webb's legacy would be measured by the NASA leadership in making Apollo the success that it was. He would also be credited with the concept that "effective government *required* administrative power." Although many today have lost sight of the man and his contributions, his efforts are still remembered at NASA. A new space telescope scheduled to be launched in space in 2013 will be named after Webb. As NASA Administrator Sean O'Keefe said when he announced the new name for the next generation space telescope, "It is fitting that Hubble's successor be named in honor of James Webb. Thanks to his efforts, we got our first glimpses at the dramatic landscape of outer space. He took our nation on its first voyages of exploration, turning our imagination into reality. Indeed, he laid the foundations at NASA for one of the most successful periods of astronomical discovery. As a result, we're rewriting the textbooks today with the help of the Hubble Space Telescope, the Chandra X-ray Observatory, and the James Webb Telescope."

It is only fitting that such a dreamer as James Webb, who in collaboration with other fellow dreamers leading such a full life of public service, would find his name in space at a time when new fellow dreamers will search the heavens for their dreams and hopes for an improved world.

Conclusion

There are those rare moments in the course of a nation's history when fellow dreamers converge and bring about great hope and benefits to humankind. From the time of our founding fathers and the birth of our nation, there have been few instances when individuals with selfless dreams have collaborated to improve the lot of others. Whether it be in civil rights, economic security for the elderly and infirm, or the rights of free democratic society, no one person can accomplish his or her dreams without the assistance of fellow dreamers. George Washington or Thomas Jefferson alone could not bring about the birth of a new nation under constitutional law. Martin Luther King, Jr. and Lyndon Baines Johnson alone could not bring about civil rights for minorities. Henry Garland Bennett or Harry S. Truman alone could not bring about a program to provide technical assistance to underdeveloped countries.

With the great national and international needs in our world today, there is a sense of urgency for fellow dreamers to unselfishly cooperate in meeting those needs. With divisions in our country and Congress, threats of terrorism looming, and the majority of the world still in impoverished conditions, will those fellow dreamers be able to provide leadership to bring hope to those in need?

There are some bright, positive signs. Prominent national and international leaders have made notable efforts at providing hope and help to those in need. Presidents Carter and Clinton have created foundations to meet human needs internationally. The Carter Center has accomplished remarkable achievements in negotiating national disputes and eradicating human disease. The Clinton Global Initiative has accomplished wonders by funding disease research and encouraging private business ventures. Entrepreneurs have established innovative programs for education and business. The Bill and Linda Gates Foundation has joined with other financiers to provide funds for education, disease research and individual business ventures. Numerous non-profit organizations continue to make an international impact on improving the human condition, including Heifer International and Doctors Without Borders. Numerous dreamers in India began a program of providing start-up capital for small business ventures. In 2006 the Norwegian Nobel Committee awarded the Nobel Peace Prize to Muhammed Yunus and Grameen Bank "for their efforts to create economic and social development from below. Lasting peace can not be achieved unless large population groups find ways to break out of poverty."

It may be of significance that national governments have been far behind such private, non-profit organizations in meeting international human needs. The demand for funding in so many other areas may limit government ability to meet the need for international programs of self-help. It is regrettable that government leaders, in some of the countries of Asia and Africa with the most needy circumstances, are the very ones preventing the availability of aid and cures to its population.

The foreign policy of our country seems to change direction with new national administrations. International events, in some cases, may leave us with little alternative in allocating our resources in international affairs. The great danger is that pressing political needs will eliminate the consideration of long-term advantages to improve the international human condition. Just as communism failed to improve the daily lives of those held in its grasp, so too, will terrorism be recognized in its inability to bring about better lives for those held in its grasp.

It is easy to be pessimistic about the national and international conditions and the ability to provide realistic help to people in need. But there is always hope that a new generation of fellow dreamers may emerge on a broad national scene to renew efforts to provide technical assistance for a needy world. Maybe a new group of fellow dreamers, such as Henry Bennett, William Holloway, Robert Kerr, Harry Truman, Haile Selassie, Benjamin Hardy and James Webb may be on the horizon to bring us hope, raise our sights and provide the leadership to meet the human needs present today. The technology, communication capabilities and knowledge of the 1950s has been improved in the areas of food production, medicine, engineering and education. The growing number of internationals being educated and trained gives us hope that unselfish leaders may be chosen to lead their countries out of misery to hope.

Just as it was with Bennett, Holloway, Kerr, Truman, Selassie, Hardy and Webb, dreams begin the process—dreams not limited because of one's birthplace or status in society; obstacles or disappointments; or the scope or challenge of the process. All of their dreams were largely unselfish, uplifting and people-oriented. Their individual dreams were able to be shared with fellow dreamers. May there be a coming together in our lifetime of such fellow dreamers.

Acknowledgments

Writing *No Little Dreams* was a unique experience for me. I learned to appreciate the hours and days spent in research and the joy of discovering new sources of information regarding the subject matter. Late in the process I was able to meet with members of Henry Garland Bennett's family. Offering fresh research materials and much encouragement, they have also been very supportive in the process of writing this book. I am especially grateful to Vera Preston-Jaeger and her husband Alan. I have missed those wonderful moments with Frances Bennett, to whom this book is dedicated. I was also fortunate to have met and interviewed Judge William Holloway, Jr., the son of the former Oklahoma Governor. Dr. Richard Poole was gracious in giving me time to share his remembrances of James Webb. In addition, I had the privilege of talking and exchanging materials with Benjamin Hardy, III, the son of Benjamin Hardy, Jr. Conrad and Joy Evans, of Stillwater, Oklahoma, offered accounts of their experiences and observation in Haile Selassie's Ethiopia. These family members and friends have all provided undisclosed materials, validating the previous research done on these men.

Others have contributed to the research for this book. Dr. James Hromas and Jim Shideler of the Oklahoma State University International Education and Outreach program have been invaluable in their encouragement and assistance with research. Amanda Hudson, Bill Welge and Jerry Hargis, at the Oklahoma History Center were also helpful in research materials. Randy Sowell and the staff at the Truman Presidential Library Archives provided valuable research assistance. Gail Martin and Peggy Lloyd, archivists at the Southwest Arkansas Regional Archives, provided personal assistance in research.

Considerable care was given by others in the proofreading and editing process for this book. My wife of 39 years, Jan, and our Missouri friend, Gaytha Suits helped with careful proofreading. Amy Sonheim provided excellent and professional assistance in editing, helping to make this a more readable book. General Doug Dollar of New Forums Press in Stillwater, Oklahoma offered great encouragement as he expressed interest early on in publishing this book.

All of these have helped me to see my dreams fulfilled. Like the fellow dreamers in this book, I am well aware that one's dreams are not fulfilled on their own. They require the encouragement, influence and support of fellow dreamers.

Appendix

Speeches

1. Henry Garland Bennett:

- "Point 4: Adventure in Education" Remarks given as Administrator of the Technical Cooperation Administration, Department of State, before the American Vocational Association Convention in Minneapolis, Minnesota, November 28, 1951—just three weeks before his tragic death in a plane crash in northern Iran
- Address to the Sixth Session of the United Nations Food and Agriculture Organization, Rome, Italy, December 4, 1951

2. William Judson Holloway:

State of the State Address before the Oklahoma State legislature in Oklahoma City, Oklahoma, on May 16, 1929

3. Robert Samuel Kerr:

Eulogy given at the funeral service for Dr. and Mrs. Henry Bennett, in Stillwater, Oklahoma, on January 5, 1952

4. Harry S. Truman

1949 Inauguration Speech introducing the Point Four program providing technical assistance to underdeveloped countries following World War II

5. Haile Selassie:

Speech given before the League of Nations in Geneva, Switzerland, on June 30, 1936

6. Benjamin Hardy:

Personal letter written to North Carolina friend

7. James Edwin Webb:

- Prepared remarks by Benjamin Hardy for Acting Secretary of State Webb for the University of North Carolina, Chapel Hill, North Carolina, on June 3, 1949;
- Remarks given following the death of Henry Bennett

"Point 4: Adventures in Education"

(Remarks by Dr. Henry G. Bennett, Administrator,
Technical Cooperation Administration, Department of State,
before the American Vocational Association in
Minneapolis, Minnesota, November 28, 1951)

Governor Anderson, President Fetterolf, Fellow Teachers, and Educators:

It is an honor and a delight to be here this evening, with old friends and colleagues. You may think of me as a black sheep who has strayed from the educational fold into a den of bureaucrats. It is exactly a year since I left Stillwater, Oklahoma to join the Point 4 Program in Washington. Believe me, I haven't gone astray. No one who has ploughed the field of education for a lifetime can escape from it, —or would wish to. For me, fortunately, no escape was necessary.

The Point 4 Program is education, from the first to the last. It is in fact the essence of education: an adventure in the sharing of knowledge; an adventure in which those who share their knowledge gain new insight and new experiences.

We in Point 4 are engaging in clearing and cultivating a new corner of the educational field. It is pioneer work. But we cannot claim to be the first on the scene. The missionaries began it, more than a hundred years ago. Almost everywhere you go in the service of Point 4 you can see traces of their work. And what you see is good.

Following in their footsteps, we are learning that this brand of education—like most others—demands patience and humility. Even more, it demands a decent respect and a genuine liking for one's fellow men. These, no less than the technical knowledge and skill, are essential ingredients of Point 4 work, if it is to achieve its purpose.

While the missionaries were its early exponents, the world-wide movement that goes by the name Point 4 today is strictly a product of the 20th Century. It could not have been conceived or carried out in the setting of the 19th or any other Century.

Point 4 is the product of two great revolutions that have arisen to shape the course of history in my lifetime. One is the development of western scientific thought and technology, actually a part of the even more significant revolution in education, which made possible the practical application of science and technology, so that millions of ordinary people could put them to daily use. I need not take the time of this audience, which numbers so many leaders, to trace the course of that revolution. But I would simply remind you of what our land grant colleges and universities, our vocational schools, and the tremendous burgeoning of American high-school education have done to bridge the gap between science and daily life, between classroom and laboratory on the one hand, and the workshop and the farm on the other.

In one respect it was a physical revolution, in terms of thousands of miles of new roads which put a school within reach of every American child. We saw one dramatic result of this physical fact when the illiteracy rate of 25 per cent among men drafted into the armed forces in World War I was dropped to 5 per cent among those drafted during World War II.

But it was even a more philosophical revolution, with democratic overtones, for it proclaimed that opportunity was still the inherent right of every American, —opportunity to create for himself a better and fuller life, and to realize his individual potentialities. So we have set the stage in this country, over the past fifty years, for the physical availability of technical as well as academic education to the ordinary man, woman and child. And we have freed education, for practical purposes, from the old philosophical straitjacket which sought to restrict it to an elite, aristocratic few and to associate it with book-learning in an ivory tower.

While we were fighting our own education battles, another revolution was brewing in parts of the world of which most Americans were only vaguely conscious. More than a billion people of Asia, Africa and Latin America, most of them bypassed by the industrial revolution of the 19th Century—and some even bypassed by the dynamic political ideas that culminated in the French and American revolutions—were waking up to the possibilities of both.

They were not only waking up—they were beginning to demand admittance to the 20th Century and access to the fruits of both revolutions. When the history of the past 50 years is written, I suspect it will be their awakening, rather than the rise of the police state in Europe that will dominate the scene. And the ferment in which we are living our lives will be traceable to the three great drives that motivate the majority of the human race today: the drives for self-government, for economic progress, and for social justice.

It will be seen that we Americans are, ourselves, partly responsible for the fact that more than a billion people are now demanding what we ourselves have demanded and have proclaimed to be the most desirable human values. For a hundred and seventy-five years we have been talking about men being created equal, about the right to life, liberty and the pursuit of happiness, about government of the people, by the people and for the people.

This is inflammatory talk. The only wonder is that it did not ignite fires of discontent and anger sooner among great masses of people afflicted with hunger, disease, and poverty.

Now I am going to say something unconventional—and that is, that communism is not primarily responsible for the growing tensions in the areas we call "underdeveloped." Communism is simply cashing in on the conditions of hunger, disease and ignorance in which more than a billion people have been held captive far too long. These people now have a window into the 20th Century, through which they can see the evidences of progress long denied to them, and through which they can hear those great ideas of self-government, economic progress and social justice that we have been championing. They are looking for a door, and we are helping them to find one. We can do no less than welcome them as partners. To do so is in our own best interest, for they are our neighbors in a shrinking world. This, in a nutshell, is the meaning of Point 4.

That is the background against which the President made his historic statement in January 1949, proclaiming, as the fourth point of American foreign policy, the vital interest of our country in the progress and well-being of more than a billion neighbors.

Today, nearly three years later, the Point 4 Program is entering its second year of life. Perhaps this is as good a time as any to stop and consider the way we may have come and the direction we expect to go.

I have said that the Point 4 Program is education. But I should add that it is not conventional education. In our work you will not find much of the teacher-pupil relationship. In this gathering, I do not need to stress the truism that education is self-education: that the only discipline worth having is self-discipline. This truth is nowhere more apparent than in the business of technical cooperation, which consists in a blending of ideas and a chemical reaction within cultures.

You might think of Point 4 cooperation as the catalytic agent that generates progress within a culture, without changing its essential character.

If we did not accept this axiom through reasoning, we would arrive at it through experience. Once it is accepted, Point 4 cooperation becomes not only possible, but remarkably fruitful. Once you know, and the people with whom you work in Asia, Africa or Latin America know that you have not come to preach democracy or to impose the American way of life, but to help them do the things they want to do, then you and they, together, can get on with the job.

Another axiom of technical cooperation is that it begins where people are. Once that is accepted, you can almost chart the course of the program.

You can assume, as we have done, that where 8 out of 10 people live on the land, and are chronically hungry because they cannot wrest a decent living from the land, cooperation begins with simple improvements in the cultivation of the soil: better seed, and better methods of sowing; better tools, plus the skill to use and maintain them; the use of resources at hand, such as fertilizer and native legumes. Can these simple things produce results? We know they can, and so, now, do the farmers of India and Liberia and Paraguay. They themselves have, in fact, produced startling results, such as the doubling of their wheat and potato yields in two or three years.

Moreover, you can assume, beginning again where people are, that when 7 out of 10 people suffer chronically from diseases that sap their strength and cut their life expectancy to 30 years, then simple health practices are a basic prerequisite to other forward steps. Add to this the fact that modern medicine has found ways to prevent most of the diseases that afflict the people of the underdeveloped areas—malaria, dysentery, typhoid, smallpox and the like—and you have a basis for concrete action.

You can attack the malaria mosquito with DDT. You can practically wipe out dysentery by boiling water and chlorinating wells. You can put an end to smallpox and other plagues by the relatively simple expedient of inoculation. When I say "you," I mean "we." For every one of these health measures begins cooperatively. Before long, however, every one is taken over by the people who benefit from it.

Finally, you can take it that all other phases of progress will wait on basic education, where 7 out of 10 members of a society never learn to read or write or have access to vocational skills beyond those known in biblical times. Accordingly, you can get busy with the organization of teacher training and the modernizing of public education systems fitted to the needs of that particular society.

I have been describing to you the major activities of the Point 4 Program in the 35 countries which are cooperating with us in the program today. Of approximately 600 American technicians now at work in those countries, about one-third are engaged in helping farmers to grow more food and helping governments to organize farm schools and extension systems. Another 200 are concerned with public health and the training of people in the prevention of disease. About a hundred are advising on the training of teachers and the establishment of schools.

Food, health and education: these three essentials have consumed the bulk of our energies and our funds in the first year of the Program. Not only are they the keys to eventual economic and social progress, but they are the things that the people of the underdeveloped areas themselves most ardently and earnestly desire. I have said that Point 4 cooperation is designed to help people do what they want to do. That is not a pious statement of policy. It is a practical rule for getting good and quick, concrete results.

And we need quick concrete results even in this long-range effort. We need the hope and enthusiasm that will sustain a long hard pull. Among people inured to hardship and privation, a better crop this year and a family free from malaria are blessings beyond price. If Point 4 can produce evidences of personal achievement and the hope they engender as well as more food and better health, it will be well on the way to success.

I have over simplified our Program for purposes of brevity. There are, of course, many other lines of work that contribute to the basic three I have mentioned. About a hundred American technicians, men and women, are serving as advisors in the development of mineral and power resources, of transportation, industry, housing, labor standards, community welfare and public administration. These activities will become more important as the Program progresses and expands.

Now I want to look ahead for a moment. The Mutual Security Act, approved by the President on October 10, provided that the Point 4 Program, should remain in the Department of State, and be coordinated with the other foreign aid programs by Mr. Averill Harriman.

The Congress gave Point 4 what was, in effect, a vote of confidence by authorizing the full amount that we thought we could spend wisely in the year ending next June 30th. The Appropriations Act confirmed our request. Out of a foreign aid program of about Seven-and-a-Quarter Billion Dollars, Point 4 is to receive about 153 Million Dollars in this fiscal year. This does not include a sum of 50 Million Dollars voted by Congress for relief and resettlement of refugees to Israel, where a Point 4 program is now getting underway.

The Congress also indicated how our budget should be spent by areas. It approved a little more than 17 Million Dollars for Latin American Republics; about 60 Million Dollars for the Middle East and the independent countries of Africa; about 65 Million Dollars in India, Pakistan, Afghanistan and Nepal, which are labeled "South Asia." Out of these area appropriations will come our contribution to the technical assistance programs of the United Nations and the Organization of American States, a contribution of 13 Million Dollars, or 60 per cent of their total budget.

If you recall that our first year's budget was about 35 Million Dollars, you will agree that the considerable expansion of the program in the second year constitutes a challenge to spend wisely and effectively. However, it is not as great a challenge as you might think. For the period of planning and negotiation with other governments was well spent, and the time for action has come. I believe the pattern of cooperation I have outlined to you tonight is sound and will stand up in the years to come.

However, we should not underestimate the difficulties that lie ahead. In so far as I have any worries, and I am not a worrying man, I am concerned that the character and integrity of Point 4, as the President expressed it and as Congress has authorized it, shall be maintained against all pressures from those who misunderstand its purpose, or understanding, do not support that purpose.

The whole trend of history, if I read it correctly, bears out the rightness of the President's Point 4 concept. It is, and must remain, a cooperative program. It is and shall remain, primarily a program of education. Our friends of the underdeveloped areas do not want charity. They want to become independent, by their own efforts, of our help and of all outside help. They are eternally right in asking us to share knowledge and skill—which cannot be <u>given</u> away—so that they may achieve self-reliance and dignity that goes with it. They represent old cultures that long pre-date ours. They would not permit us to super-impose our culture on theirs, even if we were so foolish as to try. There are many paths to progress as there are nations. They want to choose their own.

As we go about the business of Point 4 cooperation, we can do no better than to ask ourselves this question. "What makes a nation great?"

Is it the wealth of natural resources? Is it the presence of coal, iron, tin and oil underground? In this respect, the nations joined with us in the Point 4 Program are well-endowed, and it should not be too diffi-cult for them to achieve greatness within a few years. In that case, Point 4 could concentrate on development of natural resources. We should spend our energies and our funds on digging coal, iron, manga-nese, and oil out of the ground. The so-called "underdeveloped" areas would then become "developed." Their people would be given useful work. Their governments would amass national revenues. And we would get raw materials we need for our industries.

There is nothing wrong with this suggestion, except that it has not shown, by itself, that it can achieve the main purpose for which Point 4 was created; the development of strong, self-reliant, progressive soci-eties. Instead, it has too often created the kind of situation we have in Iran, where 17 million people are living in misery and want beside what is one of the richest and was one of the most efficiently tapped oil deposits in the world. Or the situation we have in Bolivia, where the miner engaged in digging out of the richest tin deposits in the world cannot afford to feed and clothe his family decently.

Moreover, I remember a little city-state, sitting on the coast of ancient Greece, whose people achieved greatness though their only natural resource was the sea on their doorstep.

So I think we link greatness with human resources—with native ability and enterprise? If this is the only clue, then the people of the "underdeveloped" areas have an equal chance in the race. They are as richly endowed as we are with intelligence and aptitude. You have only to get to know them, as I have, to realize that they are responsive to new ideas. You have only to watch Point 4 in action to sense that the challenge of hardship and poverty has made them shrewd and resourceful, if sometimes cautious in taking risks which people living close to the margin of hunger cannot afford to take.

I think there is the potential in all our Point 4 partners, as their past civilizations have testified in many cases. What then is the missing component needed to help them realize their inherent capabilities?

I think we have an answer in that one word, "Education," if we interpret the word broadly enough. The kind of education that will enable them to meet the challenge of their environment is now within their reach. It is within their reach because we in North America and Europe have found the answers to the tropical diseases that have held millions captive. We have learned in the past 50 years how to control those tropical disease. We believe they can be not only controlled, but wiped out. The techniques for wiping them out are in our hands and will be transferred to theirs. Point 4 is the agency that will make the transfer.

I think that in the next ten years you will see education perform man-made miracles. You may well see food production doubled in most of the underdeveloped nations. You are likely to see illiteracy cut in half. And you should see, if I am not mistaken, a great upsurge of energy and a flowering of native genius among people long unaccustomed to opportunity.

If I have overestimated the potential of Point 4, then all of us here tonight will have to revise our ideas about the power of education. But I, for one, have seen too many miracles in my little town of Stillwater, Oklahoma, among the young people I have known, to disbelieve in them.

I cannot share the general gloom that pervades our world today. We are living in a period of unparalleled opportunity. The Point 4 Program, by itself, —and it is a comparatively small effort—can bring hope to millions of people. Already it is offering them not only faith, but works.

Henry G. Bennett, Administrator of the Point Four Program

(Speech at Rome, Italy, November 19, 1951 at the Sixth Session of the United Nations Food and Agriculture Organization)

Mr. Chairman, delegates to the Assembly of FAO, it is indeed an honour to be privileged to speak to this distinguished group, representing as you do so many nations, coming together as you are to advance the interest of food and agriculture around the world. It is an especial privilege to me because I was honoured to be a member of the delegation from the USA at the Quebec Conference when the charter for FAO was signed. I have a priceless treasure because it was with my fountain pen that the Chairman of our delegation signed for the United States of America. From then until now, I have watched with great interest the progress made by FAO. These six years have been years of progress. Progress in many ways. First of all, I think in a physical way it is marvelous that the country of Italy has provided this great beautiful building for the permanent use of FAO. All of us are deeply indebted to them, and I share the gratitude which I know all of you feel.

Great progress has been made in the Organization round the world. To me it is a matter of pride that such competent men and women have been selected for the work of FAO in the respective countries where the work is being carried forward so well today. Progress has been made in the programs of many areas of the earth in increasing food production. In fact, all of us together can be proud of the accomplishments of FAO, but proud as we are of the achievements up to date, all of us I know must realize that we are losing the fight of increasing food production as compared with increasing population in the world. We have had the report from the Director-General that while the population of the world has grown 12% since World War II, we have increased food production only 9%, so we must face reality that we are losing the fight and it is not necessary. We can win the fight. It can be won because we have enough scientific and technical knowledge now available, if applied, to produce sufficient food to feed adequately and well all of the teeming millions of the world.

A great group of scientists and technicians in laboratories and experiment stations around the world is continually increasing our knowledge of food production, food preservation, nutrition, and distribution of food. These advances in science and technology are not the monopoly of any nation or group of nations, but are available for the use of mankind. These advances have been made possible by the contributions of all nations in the past years, and we have borrowed from all people around the world.

In livestock, we have borrowed our great beef cattle breeds from the British Isles, our dairy cattle from the Channel Islands, Switzerland, Germany, from the Low Countries, from Scotland. We have borrowed beef cattle from India; our horses from Arabia, from the Middle East, from France, from Belgium and from Spain. We have borrowed from round the world swine, and sheep. We have borrowed our poultry from everywhere. Our foundation livestock has come from all over the world to the Western Hemisphere. Not only that, we have borrowed our wheat from Turkey—Turkey Red they call it—which has been the foundation of our great wheat production.

We have borrowed grasses from Africa; melons from Africa and the Middle East; horticulture products from all over this world; our citrus fruit from the Middle East, from Spain, Italy and Brazil. Our alfalfa from Turkey and the Middle East; our clovers from Persia and Korea. From Manchuria and from North China the great crop of soy beans which has come to be a billion dollar crop each year. In turn, the Western Hemisphere has furnished to the world potatoes; sweet potatoes, the yams, the Irish potato, and tobacco. On the other hand, the American Indian furnished sugar cane, corn, maize to all mankind.

We have borrowed scientific data. We have borrowed and used in the Western world and now we come with technical assistance. It is a two-way street. We are cooperatively sharing the advances that have been made in science, technology, genetics and nutrition. And so we come, all of us together with full knowledge that none of us has come empty-handed. Every country represented has made some contribution to the sum total of our knowledge of food and food production.

By joining hands together we can win this fight and can win it in this generation. We know enough now, if this knowledge is applied to win this fight. And so I come this morning representing the United States of America, as Administrator of President Truman's Point 4 program—the Technical Cooperation Administration—and I come offering you such facilities as we have cooperatively in food and agriculture.

Your great Director-General and I have been friends for a quarter of a century. Together we are working to bring about close cooperation in our agencies. In like fashion, we join the Colombo plan. All agencies will have to work cooperatively if we can win in this hard fight to feed all mankind. We have two great problems involved: (1) How can we find a way to live together in peace; (2) How can we produce enough to feed and clothe and house and educate mankind and bring health in like fashion to all people everywhere. We come, representing as we do our agency, hoping that you will accept us, hoping that cooperatively together we may be able to achieve more than we can separately.

I have believed in FAO since its beginning. I believe in it now—in its great leadership—and I come congratulating you on the achievements made and hoping in the years ahead through education—universal for all people—all the children of all people, girls and boys alike, through experimentation and research and through extension, that we may be able to win the fight in this struggle to feed a hungry world.

I thank you, Director Dodd, and your associates for this opportunity you have given me this morning to address this distinguished group of men and women, and all of us from America come offering you the cooperation which we are ready to share to the limit of our ability. It is our hope that from time to time many of you will find it possible to visit the United States of America and when you do, if you will let us know that you are there, you will find us ready and willing to extend to you the same courtesies which you have so generously extended to us in your respective countries when we have visited you at your homes. Thank you!

State of the State Address

(Governor William Holloway, to the Oklahoma State Legislature, Oklahoma City, May 16, 1929)

(Remarks enclosed in quotation marks are impromptu references made by Governor Holloway while reading his message.)

To the Senate and House of Representatives of the Extraordinary Session of the Twelfth Legislature of the State of Oklahoma:

By virtue of the authority vested in me as Governor of the State of Oklahoma, in Section Seven of Article Six of the Constitution, this Legislature has been convened in extraordinary session upon the present occasion. It seems fitting, first, to express to each member of the Senate and of the House of Representatives my appreciation for your sincere interest manifested in the affairs of state.

In order to avoid undue sacrifice on your part and expense to the state, it is necessary to invite your attention to the consideration of the fewest possible subjects consistent with the public welfare. Therefore, the topics briefly discussed in this message are those which, in my judgment, are of paramount importance, and for which therefore is widespread and urgent demand for consideration.

In view of public needs at this time, I submit for your deliberation the following subjects which subsequently will be discussed in order:

"And you might want to write these down because I didn't have any money to have any of these messages printed, and Mr. Speaker and Mr. President, I would like to make a request of both Houses, in view of that statement, if you don't mind, I would like to have each House have printed for me personally about 300 extra copies and furnished to me—that is, copies of your Journal, if you don't mind doing that."

(1)   Appropriations

(2)	State highways
(3)	Public education
(4)	Election laws
(5)	Salaries of elected officials
(6)	Executive clemency
(7)	Fish and game
(8)	State Tax Commission
(9)	Agriculture
(10)	Court's judicial reform, and judicial procedure
(11)	Local legislation

APPROPRIATIONS

As you know, the regular session of the Twelfth Legislature was adjourned without having passed appropriations with which to defray the expenses of government during the biennium beginning July 1, 1929, and ending June 30, 1931. It is of course necessary that fiscal provision be made for the carrying on of the duties of all departments of state and for the adequate functioning of the various state institutions, penal, eleemosynary, and educational. The recommendations contained in the departmental appropriations bill which will be submitted for your consideration were arrived at by conference of the various department heads with the Appropriations Committees during the regular session, and in further conferences since that time. The institutional budgets were drawn up in conference with the heads of the institutions concerned, with the Governor, the State Budget Officer, the Chairman of the Senate Appropriations Committee, and the Chairman of the House Appropriations Committee.

Appropriations Must Not Exceed $29,000,000.00

Changes and readjustments are important and imperative, I realize, but there is not time at present to provide new sources of income to the State. Furthermore, such changes must be based upon information that can be secured only through careful and thoughtful investigation. The available revenue from all sources for carrying on the state governmental and institutional activities will, without doubt, not exceed thirty-one million dollars. Of this amount, two million dollars have already been spent, by reason of the deficit which will be brought forward with the closing of the present biennium.

"In other words, that is an approximate figure; it might go a little over two million."

After thorough investigation, I am convinced that the State government can be operated for the next two years efficiently and well on the amount remaining. Under no circumstances will I approve appropriation bills totaling more than the twenty-nine millions of dollars, believed to be available from present sources of revenue after provisions for the current deficit has been made.

STATE HIGHWAYS

Our state highways are the arteries of communication through which pulses the life blood of our commerce and industry, quickening our social life, terminating the isolation of the farm, stimulating and nourishing the prosperity of our commonwealth. Since the adequate development of our state highway system directly affects the welfare of every citizen of the State, I feel it mandatory to invite your attention to the following highway problems which, in my judgment, are urgent and pressing for solution.

Toll Bridges

It should be a fundamental policy of state highway construction and maintenance to provide free and uninterrupted traffic between all points within the state, and connection with all important centers outside of the state that have adequate highway terminals at our borders. The existence of numerous toll bridges both within the State and at its borders is an obstacle to the realization of this basic policy. The purchase by Oklahoma of intra-state toll bridges which are intimately connected with the maintenance and extension of our system of highways, as well as the joint purchase of essential inter-state toll bridges by this State and any bordering state, is necessary to the continued desirable expansion of our state highway system.

Legislation should therefore be enacted, authorizing the State Highway Commission to enter into contract for the purchase of any and all of the toll bridges within this State that may, in the judgment of the Commission, be deemed essential to the betterment of state highways. Furthermore, in the event that the Commission is not able to obtain these by contract, the State Highway Commission should be authorized to obtain such bridges by condemnation. The State's program with reference to toll bridges should not, however, be permitted to drain funds ordinarily available for the maintenance and extension of hard-surfaced and graveled highways, thus hampering the good-roads programs throughout the State as a whole. It is therefore recommended that the Highway Commission be authorized to issue bonds against such bridges, as in their judgment, it seems advisable to purchase, for sums not greater than the purchase price, such sums to be amortized through the continued operation of the bridges on a toll basis, sufficient to produce only the revenue needed for that purchase. When the total bond issue against any bridge has been amortized, it shall then and forever be a free bridge. In order that the people of this State shall have an added burden of interest to pay by reason of such a bond issue, it is further recommended that any funds of the several departments of state, or any funds subject to investment by any part of the state, be made legally available, with the approval of the boards governing such departments, for use in the purchase of such bonds. Thus, it appears to me, those using the bridges will eventually pay for them. No added burden will be imposed upon anyone, and the continued expansion of the road system throughout the State will be safeguarded.

Similarly, plenary power should be vested in the State Highway Commission to join with the lawfully authorized representatives of other states, bordering upon ours, to obtain for the public such inter-state toll bridges as may by the Commission be deemed necessary. The Highway Commission should also be authorized to join with responsible representatives of other states in constructing bridges across state lines under such terms and conditions as may to our Highway Commission seems necessary, if so doing would in their judgment better conserve the interests of Oklahoma; provided that such bridges, when obtained by joint action of own and an adjoining state, shall be thrown open to the public either as free bridges, or operated as toll bridges under joint control, with such tolls charged as may be necessary for the repayment of the purchase or building price only. It should be distinctly understood that when the total bond issue against any bridge has been paid, it shall then and forever be a free bridge.

Employees

Legislation should be enacted giving the State Highway Commission greater discretion in the employment and compensation of the Chief Engineer and the Secretary of the Commission. These positions have duties which require a high degree of technical training and proficiency, and all restrictions which may in any way hamper the Highway Commission in securing the services of the best possible men for these important appointments should, in my judgment, be removed.

Estimate and Purchase of Materials

Legislation should be enacted giving the State Highway Commission permission to purchase materials for road building or bridge construction in such quantities and at such times as may be deemed advisable to meet the demands for the fiscal year in which the purchase is made. Materials other than those needed to fill existing contracts should be purchased upon an estimate by the Chief Engineer of the Highway Commission of the quantities of each of the several materials that will be needed during the fiscal year. In making this estimate, the Chief Engineer should be limited by the estimated income available during the fiscal year and the amount of construction and repair that can be accomplished in that time.

Motor Vehicle Registration Department

Having in mind the efficiency of the State Highway Department, I recommend that this Commission be relieved of the duty now imposed upon it by the Automobile Registration Law. In my judgment, this law is primarily intended as a source of revenue and a means of identification of owners, which falls to this extent within the police power of the State and should not be imposed upon the Highway Commission.

Legislation should be enacted, establishing a department, to be known as the Motor Vehicle Registration Department, whose function should be to register motor vehicles and collect motor registration fees as required under present laws. Such a department need not increase the number of employees, and would be more efficient. Rigid rules should be provided by laws, regulating the distribution of automobile tags and the reports and money deposits of the collectors.

Inter-State License Co-Operation

The far-reaching network of Federal highways, of which our system is rapidly and increasingly becoming a part, makes it imperative that legislation be enacted immediately, permitting reciprocal recognition of automobile licenses issued by other states.

"Now, you have read much in the papers recently about the war going on between Kansas and Oklahoma. The Governor of that state and I have been trying to call a truce until something may be done in the way of legislation to relieve that situation."

Motor Bus Taxation

It is a matter of common knowledge that the business of transporting passengers and freight by motor carriers has increased by leaps and bounds, and more is taking over the traffic of interurban and urban street railways and the short haul passengers of railroads. This growth of business has been affected at the expense of other carriers that are heavy tax-payers, through the utilization of highways built by public taxation. At the present time, a bus transporting forty passengers pays the identical amount per mile that is levied against one transporting five. A mere statement of these facts, known to everybody, demonstrates the inadequacy of our system. The Motor Carrier Act found in Chapter 113, Session Laws of 1923, should be amended in such manner as to require these carriers to pay a tax more nearly in keeping with the burdens of constructing and maintaining the highways from which they derive their prosperity.

State Road Bond Issue

There seems to be a growing and urgent demand for a road bond issue that will quickly meet the needs of the State for a complete hard-surfaced highway system. You would be unwilling, if my judgment is correct, to act upon this matter until there has first been made a comprehensive and all-inclusive survey of the entire state that will graphically reveal just what is needed. The expenditure of one hundred million dollars is too colossal a task to be entered into hurriedly and without adequate data upon which to fund a definite program. Such an amount is about four times that usually contained in the total biennial appropriations. It is well worthy of the most careful and undivided attention of a legislature.

It is possible that the necessary data may be available before the adjournment of the extraordinary session. In that event, you would be in position to carry through that thorough and comprehensive consideration of the facts involved which you yourselves would require, and which our citizens would expect before the project of a bond issue could be entertained.

If, on the other hand, such data as is necessary can not be compiled before your adjournment, when such an investigation as that suggested above has been made and the actual needs and costs have been determined, and if it seems to be the concensus of opinion of the citizenry of the State that such an undertaking be entered into, I will then convoke another extra session for that sole purpose. No citizen should be willing to launch upon so far-reaching a road-building program as is contemplated in the bond issue discussed until he is thoroughly informed and has all the facts at his disposal.

PUBLIC EDUCATION

Government has no function transcending in importance the education of its citizens, and no phase of our society changes more rapidly than education. Because there have been no major changes in the laws affecting public school support and administration since the inception of statehood, certain readjustments are now pressing. Your attention is respectfully invited to the following suggestions and recommendations which I consider to be at the present time most urgent.

Public School Support

Financial inequalities of the school districts make it impossible for them to support uniform school programs. An almost inconceivable difference exists among districts as to their ability to support an adequate program. Inasmuch as the people in these school districts are doing all that is possible according to the law, they must depend upon the Legislature of Oklahoma to provide the solution to this problem. Past legislatures have appropriated state funds to supplement their inadequate local revenue. Due to such factors as the constantly enlarged enrollment in the public schools, the increase in the number of high schools, the longer term, and the concentration of wealth in certain centers, the number of weak school districts in Oklahoma is increasing. In spite of the fact that conditions today are markedly different from those prevailing at statehood, this great commonwealth still attempts to maintain its schools under the provisions of the same statutes and by the same method of taxation which were at that time set up.

The State Legislature, during the regular session, passed Senate Bill No. 52, supplementing the regular appropriation for the aid of weak schools. This bill carried an appropriation of $500,000. Because of a deficit in the revenues of the State for the current fiscal year, it was necessary to veto this bill. Such action was taken with reluctance and profound regret. Nevertheless, I stand committed to the policy of keeping the channels of opportunity open to every boy and girl within our borders. It is imperative that a state as rich and as prosperous as the great State of Oklahoma should guarantee equity of chance to all of its children. The State should provide for such an education as will best fit the young for the increasingly complex duties and responsibilities of citizenship and the ever more difficult task of earning a living. The time must never come in Oklahoma when education will be an accident of birth or of residence, or the privilege of the economically fortunate. The time has come, however, when we must face this problem squarely and settle it once and for all. I realize that you may be too pressed to make a thorough and comprehensive survey of all available revenues as a basis for the enactment of remedial legislation. Yet, it seems to me that the Twelfth Legislature should give this vital school problem the most serious and careful consideration, to limited time available, toward eliminating the inequities of educational opportunity now existing within our State.

A State System of Higher Education

Higher education—"This is a subject which is becoming serious as well as the aid necessary for the weak school districts of Oklahoma"—is in Oklahoma largely a state enterprise. We maintain eighteen tax-supported institutions for higher learning, which enroll approximately 80 per cent of all college students in the State. These schools have been created and have developed with no definite plan and with no correlating agency to promote cooperation and unity of function and to prevent needless duplication and competition. As a natural consequence of this unregulated growth, constantly multiplying problems involving duplication of curriculum and of effort have arisen. It is evident that there can be no permanent solution of the State's higher education difficulties until the issues are squarely faced and the State assumes responsibility for determining an intelligent plan for the future development of its colleges. The acceptance of the following principles seems to be essential before a state system of higher education can in reality be established:

1. All state institutions for higher education are parts of a single state system.
2. The sole object of the system is to serve the state economically and effectively.
3. Where several state institutions have been established and their func-

tions defined, no one institution should attempt to cover the entire field of higher education.

4. No institution should attempt to offer a particular course of study when it can be shown that greater benefit to the state would result if that particular curriculum were offered in another school.

5. State service can better be accomplished by friendly cooperation than by competition and rivalry. "There is no excuse for a spirit of competition developing among the higher institutions of learning in the State of Oklahoma. The only thing we want to consider is the welfare of all the people in this state; that is all! We are not trying to build up anything for any individual nor any town in this state, but we have the problem of unifying the policy for higher education in this state."

6. Since an institution's only excuse for existence is the service it can render, the final test of its function is to determine the way in which it best can serve the state. "Now, I am not just going to offer you a lot of general suggestions and then leave you in the woods. I am going to offer you some practical suggestions as the basis for intelligent consideration, because you haven't the time, in four or five weeks, to make an exhaustive and intelligent study of these great problems. And, don't think this is entirely from my study either. I have had some of the ablest men in this state work on this for some seven or eight weeks, and here is what I am going to recommend."

To vitalize these principles and thereby bring about a unified state system of higher education, legislation should be enacted incorporating the following proposals:

1. The number of governing boards for state institutions for higher learning should be reduced from nine to three:

   a. The Board of Regents of Oklahoma University should control the State University. This Board was established by the Eleventh Legislature, and should be made permanent by constitutional amendment. "So that when a Board is appointed, members thereof cannot be removed except for cause, and serious cause at that."

   b. The Board of Regents for the Agricultural and Mechanical Colleges of the State should control all State agricultural and vocational schools. In order to establish a separate Board of Regents for the Agricultural and Mechanical Colleges, it will be necessary to amend the second paragraph of Article six, Section 31, of the State Constitution. I consider that such an amendment is imperative, and its adoption would mean much to the future growth and welfare of our great Agricultural and Mechanical College. "Now I hope it will not develop a feeling that in trying to establish a Board of Regents for that institution, and thereby taking away its immediate control from the State Board of Agriculture, that it is any effort on the part of anybody to make it any less an agricultural college. I know that some persons in the state have been spreading propaganda that that is the purpose for which this amendment is being pushed forward and urged in this state. But I want to say to you that the Board of Agriculture is appointed by the Governor and can be removed in a moment's time by him, and it is not right that a great educational institution of this state should have a Board of Regents so fixed by the Constitution that any Governor it matters not what his purpose might be, can throw an institution like that into chaos overnight. I hope that this Legislature will submit that question to the people of this state, because I believe when it is fairly presented that the people of this state will overwhelmingly adopt such a constitutional amendment."

c. The State Board of Education, "—Now I am going to step on somebody's toes, but I can't help it, because I think I am right—" the only strictly educational board provided by the Constitution for the control over education, should govern all institutions of higher education maintained by the State which are not specifically mentioned above. "In other words, a Board of Regents for the A. & M. College, a Board of Regents for the University of Oklahoma and one more, a State Board of Education to control every other institution of higher learning in this state. Now, if you can imagine any reason for a separate Board of Regents for example for the School for Women at Chickasha, for the school at Wilburton, for the school at Miami, for the school at Claremore, and for all of these other institutions, any sound educational policy for them, I can't imagine what it is. You are never going to have a fixed policy in this state, unless you have fewer boards and you have to unify those boards. Why, the institutions of higher educations in Oklahoma have grown up like mushrooms overnight, every institution with its own separate board; every one in its own sphere; no co-relation with the institution over yonder or yonder, and I think it would be the greatest step forward in an educational way, if you reduce all of these boards to the three boards I have outlined here."

2. A central coordinating agency should be established for the purpose of definitely unifying the tax-supported institutions into a state system of higher education. This agency might be expected to accomplish the following results:

   a. The assembling of exact information that will show the actual costs of education at the several institutions, together with the immediate and future needs of each school, thereby giving a more accurate basis to the Governor for recommending and the Legislature for making appropriations:

   b. The checking of the up-grading and expanding tendency by a clear interpretation and definition of the function of each of the several institutions and the elimination of unnecessary and undesirable duplications;

   c. The bringing about of harmonious working relationships among the institutions by the establishment of needed councils;

   d. The unifying of the tax-supported institutions into a state system of higher education through the determination of an intelligent plan for their future development.

3. The central co-ordinating agency thus provided might well be composed of the Chairman of the State Board of Education, the Chairman of the University Board of Regents, the Chairman of the Board of Regents of the Agricultural and Mechanical Colleges, the President of the University of Oklahoma, the President of the Oklahoma Agricultural and Mechanical College, a President of one of the State Teacher's College who shall have been designated by the Council of State Teacher's College Presidents, and a President of one of the other institutions who shall have been designated by the State Board of Education. These men are already in the service of the State and would receive no additional compensation.

It is not the purpose of the above proposals to place all of the state institutions of higher learning in the same class or on the same level, but rather the purpose is to avoid unnecessary and expensive duplication of curricula and effort and definitely to unify the tax-supported institutions in Oklahoma into a state system of higher education. Oklahoma is able and willing to maintain adequate facilities for higher education, but it is unable to continue indefinitely the present unregulated system.

Textbook Commission

The interests of our common schools throughout the State will best be conserved, it seems to me, by certain changes in present laws governing the selection of textbooks. The abrupt and almost complete change in textbooks every five years, as is now required, works an undue hardship upon the parents who buy the books, upon the children who use them, and upon the teachers who administer the school work in the class room. To remedy this situation, it is recommended that the following provisions be made: First, that a permanent textbook commission be authorized composed of persons technically qualified to pass upon the merits of the textbooks submitted; second, that not more than 20% of the books be changed in any one year. The serial plan of textbook adoption is in operation in many of the most progressive states and conforms to the best current practice in education throughout the nation.

"Now, a great many of us used to be school teachers, but it has been so long that we don't know very much about it any more.

"I invite you and request you to get in touch with your County Superintendent, with your State Superintendent, with your City Superintendent and with the teachers of your school systems at home, and I will venture that in nine cases out of ten they will tell you it is an abominable method now used in changing abruptly in one year practically all of the books that the children have to buy and use.

"In three-fourths of the state of this Union the serial plan of textbook adoption is now in vogue, and evidently it is in line with the best educational thought in America. Therefore, I recommend it to you for your earnest consideration, in order that present conditions may be bettered, in the interest of the people that have to buy these books.

"There is another thing upon which many do not agree with me, but with reference to which I believe I am right.

"In my judgment, the Governor should not be member of this commission. In the first place, his duties are too heavy to permit him to give the necessary time; and in the second place, the adoption of textbooks is a technical matter requiring the services of specialists. The State Superintendent of Public Instruction, on the other hand, should in my judgment remain a member.

"Now, I used to teach school from 1910 to 1914, and from 1914 up to this good hour I haven't seen inside of a textbook. Now, what in the world would I know about adopting textbooks, and what I say about myself applies to every Governor that ever sat in the Governor's office in Oklahoma.

"Now, what good excuse is there to leave the Governor upon this commission? Why should it not be best for the children of this state and for the people to permit an intelligent, efficient expert to be appointed on that board?

"Therefore, I sincerely want you, in tackling this problem, to re-constitute that commission and leave the Governor off of it.

"Now, I know as well as it is humanly possible to know that there is three times as much work already on the Governor as he can do. You fellows know that as well as I do. Don't add any more burdens. If anything ought to be done, some of the burdens ought to be taken away from the Governor.

"Therefore, I earnestly recommend that you tackle this problem immediately, because the textbooks must be adopted and secured sixty days prior to the opening of school next September, if the children are to get their books on time."

In view of the fact that there is some uncertainty as to the legal status of the present adoptions, it is imperative that the Legislature give immediate attention to these proposals.

"Now, when we repealed the text book law for free textbooks in 1925, some way or other a provision or form of amendment got into the Act, which provided in effect that the present adoptions should be good for five years from that date.

"You and I know that it was not the intention of that Legislature to pass any Act that would have for its purpose the extension of contracts. That is not sound business policy, and this Legislature should repeal that provision so that there will be no legal uncertainty about the status of the present adoption."

Certification of Teachers

In the interest of increased efficiency and economy of the admin-istration of the common schools of the State, and consonant with best practice in the most progressive States of the Union, legislation should be enacted vesting in the State Board of Education the sole power to certificate teachers for the public schools of Oklahoma.

"That is in line with educational progress and development. I say to you that I happen to know that the County Superintendents think it is best that that authority be vested wholly in the State Board of Education.

"Now, here is a subject which I am going to recommend at which I do not wish you to become frightened before you have given it thought."

County Board of Education

Many fine qualities of democracy which should not be lost are inherent in our local district system, with responsibility reposed in local citizens elected as school district officers. Consequently, the local district organization should not be changed. The very important office of County Superintendent of Public Instruction, however, should be removed from the field of partisan politics. This can be done by creating a County Board of Education, vested with the power to select the County Superintendent on a purely non-sectarian and non-partisan basis, in keeping with minimum requirements and standards to be set up by the State Board of Education. The County Board of Education should be charged also with certain powers and duties not conflicting with those now abiding in the local districts and officers.

"In other words, I think you can take, as an already established, fixed elected bunch of officials, your local Trustees, in an annual meeting and let them select in some manner a County Board of Education, and then that County Board of Education select the County Superintendent. Your County Superintendent has no excuse on earth for being elected, any more than you elect a City Superintendent by popular vote— not a bit on earth. The principles and rules are the same, and the logic is the same. It should be taken out of partisan politics, with the hope that you can get the best qualified man or woman for that important post and not just the best hand-shaker to get elected County Superintendent to have charge of our local schools."

Safeguarding School Funds

When the law providing for independent school districts was enacted, the Legislature inadvertently failed to provide for safeguarding the public funds of these districts, in that it is not mandatory for the treasurers to be under bond. This costly oversight has resulted in the loss of more than a million dollars to independent school districts during the past few years. Good business judgment demands that safeguards be thrown about all public school funds, as is now done with public money handled by treasurers of the various counties.

Vocational Education Board

The State Department of Vocational Education should be made an integral part of the State Department of Education and should be governed directly by the State Board of Education. This plan has been adopted in more than three-fourths of the states. The consolidation of this Department with the State Department of Education will eliminate one board; will provide for greater economy of operation; will make this department responsible to an elected state official rather than to an ex-officio board; and, by a co-ordination of efforts, will no doubt provide greater efficiency in this department.

"There is another off-shoot in our scheme of education, which is just out there doing the best it can. It is under an efficient ex-officio board, it is true, but if there is no reason why it should fall under the classification of one of the three boards, then it ought to be put here."

ELECTION LAWS

Popular government, in order to prevail, must provide adequate methods for the clear expression of the will of the majority. It is therefore our duty to seek out obvious defects in our present laws, and to apply such amendments and remedies as would seem to promote and effect this end.

Among the more obvious of these defects, in my judgment, are those growing out of our present laws governing the machinery of primary elections, and the present manner and method of securing a recount, as well as the contesting of elections.

Run-Off Primary

The purpose of our laws governing primary elections is to enable voters of each party to choose their candidates for public office. It was undoubtedly the hope and intention of the framers of our primary election law to secure for each of the political parties the strongest candidate from the material available. But the law as it now stands has failed to do this. At present, when three or more candidates are on the same party ticket, it is possible for one of them to be nominated by a decided minority of the party because of the majority being divided between two stronger men, either one of who could have commanded a majority had the other not been in the field. We are therefore confronted today with a primary election system which may place upon our tickets as nominees persons who do not represent the popular choice of the voting strength of their several political parties. This regrettable situation should be corrected to insure that each candidate who goes before the voters in the general election shall have been selected by a popular majority within his own party.

Legislation should therefore be enacted providing that, in case there is in any primary an office for which no candidate has received nomination by a clear majority of his party voting, a second, or run-off primary shall be held as soon after the first primary election as you deem practicable. In this run-off primary, the two candidates who received the highest number of votes cast in the first primary election should have their names placed upon the ballots of their respective parties. It is of course obvious that the above provision for a run-off primary should apply only to those instances where a clear majority was not secured by any candidate.

Contests and Recounts

The preservation of the integrity of the ballot is one of our highest duties. This integrity is threatened by reason of the fact that at present our statutes do not provide a simple, speedy, and certain method for the recount of votes in cases where unsuccessful contestants for public office honestly feel and earnestly assert the prevalence of fraud, improper methods, or incorrect results in the total vote cast at either a primary or a general election. A plain, easily understood, and adequate procedure should be provided to right this situation.

SALARIES OF ELECTED OFFICIALS

The salaries of the elected officials of the State were fixed, in most cases, nearly a quarter of a century ago under conditions vastly different from those obtaining at present. While in many instances these salaries were fair and adequate at the time, they have become, due to the increased cost of living, wholly inefficient to maintain the various state officials and their families in a city which has more than tripled in size. It is my earnest recommendation that the salaries of these officials be carefully scrutinized by you and readjusted more nearly in line with present day living costs. This seems to me a vital matter. The State cannot long continue to secure the services of able, competent, and well-trained men and women, regardless of the honor which attaches to the office, if the honorarium is not consonant with the responsibilities entailed and intelligence required for the satisfactory performance of the duties involved. By providing adequate salaries for public officials, the State gets better public servants and more efficiency in governmental operations.

"Now, let me tell you this: If you don't think it is a big task to select competent men and women on the present salaries that are provided for these posts, you simply haven't become aware of it, because you haven't had to try to do it yourself. I have offered one position to five different men in this state, all of whom have turned it down because of the salary paid. I want to tell you that when you pay your public officials an honest, reasonable figure, you are going to go a far step forward in keeping public officials away from temptation.

"It is an actual fact that I shall have to live far more economically as Governor of the State than I did as Lieutenant Governor. That is a fact. And yet, I am forced to try and live on that salary.

"Now, it is true that I will not get any benefit from this. In fact, there ought to be a specific provision put into it that it shall not be effective until two years, and commence when the new officials take office, so that there will be no misunderstanding and no feeling that this is being urged so that any public official may try to get the advantage of it at this time.

"In a few days I am going to recommend to you a reorganization of several state departments, with an increase in salary, because I am telling you now I can't even keep some of those who have promised to start work unless those salaries can be increased.

"I have offered the position of Secretary of the School Land Commission, by permission of the Board, to five different men in this state in the last two or three days. We are not going to offer it to just any Tom, Dick and Harry, I am telling you. We will let it go vacant if we can't get someone that we feel competent to do the work.

"Now, this is serious business, my friends. We must tackle these problems in that way. There are several departments of this state where the officials are appointed. The salaries ought to be increased so that we can keep some of these we have and secure others who are competent and efficient.

"Now, you will make a mistake if, under my recommendation, you try at this session of the Legislature to pass a comprehensive salary bill, raising the salaries of all appointive officials. You will wind up getting nothing through, so I hope and pray when I do submit that to you, if you think it is right and ought to be done, that you will just confine yourselves to the things I point out to you. I am pointing them out to you because of my two month's experience here, and I know we must have some help if the people's business is to be run as it should be. My friends, you and I are charged with that important responsibility, and I think we ought to meet it without regard to partisan politics, without regard to what might be popular or unpopular, and look to the welfare of the people of the State and try to put the state's business upon a high-class, honorable plane, so that all good citizens will say Amen and Well Done."

EXECUTIVE CLEMENCY

"This is a nightmare to most anybody, but it is not bothering me much, because I refuse to permit it to bother me."

The judicious and proper granting of executive clemency is one of the most serious problems with which the Governor has to deal. The wise and just exercise of this power is vital to the welfare of every citizen of the State. Limitation of the power of the Governor in respect to this should be effected by a constitutional amendment creating a board which would advise with and assist him in determining any major act of clemency. It should be possible for the Governor to grant any pardon or parole without the concurrence of the majority of the Pardon and Parole Board as expressed in a formal vote, although the power should still rest in the Governor to veto any recommendation of clemency.

"In other words, he couldn't grant an act of clemency unless the majority agreed with him and after all of them voted for it, he would still have the right to say 'no'."

I shall not ask the Legislature to pass any law concerning this matter at the present, since a statutory board so created could only be advisory under the present constitutional provisions. I contemplate making such rules and regulations as will best cope with the situation until the Constitution can be amended. A thorough examination into the merits of each case and the combined judgment of such a Board will no doubt be of tremendous assistance to the Governor, will give the convict fair consideration, and will be a protection to society.

"Therefore, I want you to submit a Constitutional amendment which, in your wisdom and judgment, will limit the power of the governor in granting executive clemency."

FISH AND GAME

You will find that there are a few minor amendments which should be made in the laws relating to fish and game, which will add to the efficient functioning of that department.

A STATE TAX COMMISSION

It is apparent to all that a complete and thorough analysis of the tax laws of the State of Oklahoma should be made in order to equalize assessments and to include certain types of property now escaping taxation. The method and manner of assessing taxes needs to be revised. A Commission, consisting of able experts only, should be created and provided with ample powers, whose sole purpose should be to make an exhaustive investigation of this matter and to prepare a report including definite recommendations, which shall be submitted to the next session of the Legislature. Adequate appropriations should be made for the maintenance of this Commission, so that its work may be comprehensive and effective. It is not the purpose of this recommendation to add to the burden of any class, but to enable the next Legislature to set up general standards so that all may bear a just share in the costs of government.

"Now, you may say this: 'We have had tax commissions before and they didn't do any good.'

"It all depends on whether you are trying to appoint a commission just to give some man a job, or whether you are really going to exercise your good judgment and pick men who will know how to do the work.

"If you provide such a commission I will guarantee you to pick the ablest men, either in Oklahoma or the United States, that we can find, if you provide money enough to do it.

"Now, there is a lot of property in Oklahoma escaping taxation— million of dollars worth of property. Now, will it be the purpose of the Legislature just to provide more funds and bring in more money to provide more jobs for more folks? That is not the thing. We ought not enlarge the offices of government any more than is absolutely necessary and consistent with honest business and good, sound efficiency;

but we can find these fellows who are escaping taxation, bring them into court, put them on the tax rolls and that will help decrease the farmers' taxes and the taxes of the average citizen of the state whose taxes are now a burden."

AGRICULTURE

Agriculture is a major industry in Oklahoma, creating between three and four hundred millions of dollars of new wealth annually in this State, and supporting directly a major portion of our population. No other single industry affects so many lives nor produces so much wealth for us. Fostering and encouraging the diverse activities of agriculture is therefore of supreme importance to the State. It must never be forgotten that Oklahoma is in competition with other states in the Union in economic agricultural production. If we do not work out our problems, we are going to increase our handicap and eventually place ourselves at serious disadvantages in the production and marketing of agricultural products. Our research in agriculture is at present far behind. I therefore wish to invite your consideration to it specifically, and believe at least three topics to be of such grave importance as to require definite discussion herein.

Soil Erosion

According to reliable Oklahoma agricultural experts, more than a million acres of arable land in this State have within the past few years been lost to production through soil erosion. This waste has been so serious that the Federal Government has allotted this State twenty thousand dollars annually to be spent for the purpose of finding the best means of conserving the fertility of the soil. These Federal funds are available when they have been matched by an equal amount from State funds. If the situation is serious enough for the Federal government to take action, I deem it my duty to recommend that these funds be made available in order that this worthy project can be effectively consummated.

Boll Weevil Investigation

The boll weevil continues to be a destructive pest in our cotton fields, causing annual losses of almost incredible magnitude. To study this pest and further its eradication in Oklahoma, the Federal government has allotted the sum of ten thousand dollars annually. This amount likewise should be matched by the State in the furtherance of this badly needed investigation and demonstration of the best methods of boll weevil control. No project could be more vital to the welfare of the farmers of southern and eastern Oklahoma than this one.

"Colonel Leecraft, you ought to get that thing through this House, because you and I are going to starve to death down there if we don't exterminate the boll weevil. Clark Wason, Colonel Leecraft and John McDonald there are especially familiar with those conditions and you should convince these fellows that that should be done."

The Dairy Industry

The dairy industry is growing rapidly in every section of this State, and is becoming one of our most profitable farm enterprises. This rapid expansion has brought to our farmers many new problems which cannot be met by the agencies at present existing. Funds should be provided for the employment of a sufficient number of dairy specialists to foster intelligently and to encourage the dairy industry in every section of the State. For, after all, in diversification by the farmer lies his most reasonable hope for a stable and profitable income, and the success of every citizen is in large measure dependent upon the success of this primary industry.

COURTS, JUDICIAL REFORM, AND JUDICIAL PROCEDURE

In response to strong public demand for changes in our laws pertaining to courts, judicial reform, and judicial procedure, I deem it my duty to open this subject for your consideration. Since I have not had time to give this matter intensive study, no specific recommendations have been formulated affecting this topic. Many of the ablest lawyers of the State are themselves at a loss to know what should be done to strengthen the service of our courts and to facilitate the trial of cases to their ultimate consummation. Many of our citizens feel that different method should be found of selecting our judiciary. The subject of our judiciary system is therefore presented to you with the earnest hope that the remedies may be found and incorporated in our laws.

LOCAL LEGISLATION

All local bills which have been properly advertised as required by laws may be given consideration by this extraordinary session.

In conclusion, may I emphasize that the best interests of the State will be conserved by a prompt and expeditious handling of the matters to come before the legislature. Imbued as I know you are with a desire to see the best interests of the State conserved and furthered, I feel sure that you will expedite the business before you to greatest extent consistent with its efficient and thorough prosecution. With these high purposes in view, I am happy to extend to you my sincerest good wishes for a pleasant and useful session here assembled, and to assure you of the fullest co-operation of the office of Governor.

W. J. Holloway,
Governor

Senator Robert S. Kerr's Remarks at the Bennett Rites,

From the January 10, 1952, Stillwater Daily News-Press Stillwater, Oklahoma

We have the feeling that as we gather here two of Oklahoma's best loved are back at home. Henry Garland Bennett and his wife, Vera Connell Bennett, will walk no more where we walk, nor smile again into the faces of those they adored and by whom they were cherished but in the hearts and minds of their family, and their associates, and the countless hosts of loving friends, they will never die.

The ground is smoother where they walked. The air is brighter and warmer where they lived, and our lives are richer and fuller today and in the future because our lives have been forever enriched by our association with and friendship for them.

Since their passing, I have thought often of a verse of scripture dear to both of them: "He hath showed thee, O man, what is good; and what doth the lord require of thee, but to do justly and to love mercy, and to walk humbly with thy God?" Micah 6.8. Dr. and Mrs. Bennett not only loved that verse of scripture, their lives were and will ever be constant reminders that we can live those words as well as speak them.

Dr. Henry Bennett became known and revered by literally countless thousands of people around the world. He and his great wife were friends and neighbors here in Stillwater, on the campus of A&M college, and to men and women, boys and girls across the length and breadth of Oklahoma. Yet, no matter where he went, his thoughts and mind would ever turn to Oklahoma. As the sunflower's face follows the sun in its journey across the heavens, so Henry Bennett's mind would turn to the State and the school and the home and the friends he loved the best. His vision was unlimited as an Oklahoma sky. His courage as boundless as her horizons; his loyalty as steadfast as the roots of her forests, and his devotion as constant as the fertility of her soil.

Dr. Bennett was a builder. He left the knocking and the tearing down to others. They had no place in him. Henry Bennett encouraged and inspired the good in others. He believed that if the heart was full of love, it had no room for hate. If it were filled with courage, it would not tolerate fear. If it were overflowing with faith, it had no room for doubt.

Henry Bennett wanted to make things grow and multiply abundantly, and he did. He knew that plants and trees lived and flourished on the elements of fertility in the soil. Therefore, he loved the soil and studied it and understood it. He believed in using it, and at the same time rebuilding and conserving it in order that it might be as productive in the future as it had been in the past. He knew and believed in, and preached the first verse of the Twenty-Fourth Psalm: "The earth is the Lord's and the fullness thereof; the world, and they that dwell therein." Therefore, he cherished both the earth and the people who lived upon it.

He loved institutions that helped to build better people. He thrilled in planning them and thrived in making realities of his plans. He knew how to build a great school and he built it. He breathed into it the breath of life of his own dynamic spirit, and it took root and grew and flourished. He had the capacity to dream glorious dreams, and then he had the magic to make those dreams come true.

He loved Oklahoma. He knew it was as fine and strong, and as magnificent as any State. He knew that Oklahoma's boys and girls, young men and young women were unexcelled on the earth. He wanted them to have schools as good and the best, and he, Dr. Henry Garland Bennett, more than any other man of his generation, led Oklahoma's gallant and noble people in providing schools as good as the best for their youth. His noblest effort was here at Stillwater. He traveled in every state and many foreign lands. He saw at first hand their best colleges and universities.

Then he set out to build here one that would equal and excel the best he saw. How well he succeeded is now a matter of history. A hundred years from now men will still be making pilgrimages here to study and learn what he did and how it was done in order that they may improve what they have. However, what you see here, grand as it is, is not the finished product. A quarter of a century from now his successors will still be making improvements and enlargements here in accordance with Bennett's master plan. And Bennett's matchless spirit will still be inspiring and giving courage to those who build and those who work, and to every student who studies here.

His was a personality which can never die. Yet, he was as humble and gracious as the lowest disciple of Christian living. He has as much confidence, yet as little arrogance as any man I ever knew. He had boundless faith in God and he had a dauntless courage inspired and sustained by that faith. He believed that all men were sons of God and his brothers. Therefore, he loved his fellow man. These are the things which led him in the fullness of his mature years and strength and power to undertake new tasks and to seek new fields.

Tennyson, in his great poem "Ulysses," tells us that a distinguished son of ancient Greece at a time when most men were seeking retirement, gave expression to his dauntless spirit in these words: "Push off my mates, and sitting well in order, smite the surrounding furrows for my purpose holds to sail beyond the sunset and all the western stars until I die." Dr. Bennett had a similar vision and an equal courage. This led him to accept the appointment from the President of the United States as Director of his country's Point 4 Program. The Program was for the technical improvement of the underdeveloped area of the earth. It was conceived as a means to help underprivileged people around the world to help themselves. Dr. Bennett gave his conception of it in these words: "The program we have described to Congress and to the public is a simple, down-to-earth, self-help program designed primarily to assist other peoples increasing their food production, bettering their health conditions, and improving their educational systems." Dr. Bennett believed that this Program was a most effective method to carry out the great commission of Jesus Christ when he said: "Go ye in all the world and preach the gospel unto every creature." And Dr. Bennett believed the other words of that Commission: "Lo, I am with you always, even unto the end of the world."

And then, he believed that Point 4 confirmed with the spirit of the Master. He believed that it was a manifestation of practical Christianity to work among people who needed help and who could find a more abundant life through it. He believed it was the strongest force for peace ever created by any government. He believed it was the most powerful weapon against Communism he had ever seen. And with his boundless faith, his restless energy, and his dauntless courage, he was making that great Program work.

He persuaded the Congress to give him authority and the money to launch it in such a way that it could reach the uttermost parts of the earth. I saw him before a great committee of the Senate. It was a fine and yet as tough a committee as I ever saw. Yet he captivated its members and won their unanimous support. I saw him with the President of the United States. He showed the President that he knew as much about the President's Program and what it could do as the President did himself. I saw him with the Secretary of State and his great staff of able and vigorous men. In a little while they learned that he knew as much or more of the job they had given him to do than they did. I talked with him before he started and as he would return from his trips abroad to South America, or Africa or Asia. Always he was the same dynamic, confident, courageous, yet humble friend. He was just as kind and humble, yet just as forthright and vigorous as when he was teaching a country school or serving as Superintendent of the schools of Choctaw County.

He knew he had come from the soil and no matter how far he traveled he never left it nor did he ever lose its undiminished energy and power.

He lived and worked in Oklahoma until he became a part of it and it a part of him, and he brought that with him to Washington, and he kept and cherished it deep in his soul as he journeyed around the world.

It is our purpose and our wish today to honor Dr. and Mrs. Bennett, but in reality, we honor ourselves. As we contemplate the lives of these noble people, we, ourselves are enriched. As we yearn in our hearts to be the source of blessing to them, we are conscious that we, rather than they, are being blessed. And it is wonderful to realize they would have it so because in life they lived for and blessed others. So successful were they that for all of the days of their lives and for all the years that men and women will be working for and loving humanity and building Oklahoma, Henry and Vera Bennett will be remembered, and what they did will be inspiring and blessing us and others.

Reproduced by TCA, Public Affairs Section, 1/22/52

"Inaugural Address"

(Remarks President Harry S. Truman,
at the United States Capitol, January 20, 1949)

Mr. Vice President, Mr. Chief Justice, fellow citizens:

I accept with humility the honor which the American people have conferred upon me. I accept it with resolve to do all that I can for the welfare of this Nation and for the peace of the world.

In performing the duties of my office, I need the help and the prayers of every one of you. I ask for your encouragement and for your support. The tasks we face are difficult. We can accomplish them only if we work together.

Each period of our national history has had its special challenges. Those that confront us now are as momentous as any in the past. Today marks the beginning of not only of a new administration, but of a period that will be eventful, perhaps decisive, for us and the world.

It may be our lot to experience, and in a large measure bring about, a major turning point in the long history of the human race. The first half of this century has been marked by unprecedented and brutal attacks on the rights of man, and by the two most frightful wars in history. The supreme need of our time is for men to learn to live together in peace and harmony.

The peoples of the earth face the future with grave uncertainty, composed almost equally of great hopes and great fears. In this time of doubt, they look to the United States as never before for good will, strength, and wise leadership.

It is fitting, therefore, that we take this occasion to proclaim to the world the essential principles of the faith by which we live, and to declare our aims to all peoples.

The American people stand firm in the faith which has inspired this Nation from the beginning. We believe that all men have a right to equal justice under the law and equal opportunity to share in the common good. We believe that all men have a right to freedom of thought and expression. We believe that all men are created equal because they are created in the image of God.

From this faith we will not be moved.

The American people desire, and are determined to work for, a world in which all nations and all peoples are free to govern themselves as they see fit, and to achieve a decent and satisfying life. Above all else, our people desire, and are determined to work for, peace on earth—a just and lasting peace—based on genuine agreement freely arrived at by equals.

In pursuit of these aims, the United States and other like-minded nations find themselves directly opposed by a regime with contrary aims and a totally different concept of life.

That regime adheres to a false philosophy which purports to offer freedom, security, and greater opportunity to mankind. Misled by that philosophy, many peoples have sacrificed their liberties only to learn to their sorrow that deceit and mockery, poverty and tyranny, are their reward.

That false philosophy is communism.

Communism is based on the belief that man is so weak and inadequate that he is unable to govern himself, and therefore requires the rule of strong masters.

Democracy is based on the conviction that man has the moral and intellectual capacity, as well as the inalienable right, to govern himself with reason and justice.

Communism subjects the individual to arrest without lawful cause, punishment without trial, and forced labor as the chattel of the state. It decrees what information he shall receive, what art he shall produce, what leaders he shall follow, and what thoughts he shall think.

Democracy maintains that government is established for the benefit of the individual, and is charged with the responsibility of protecting the rights of the individual and his freedom in the exercise of those abilities of his.

Communism maintains that social wrongs can be corrected only by violence.

Democracy has proved that social justice can be achieved through peaceful change.

Communism holds that the world is so widely divided into opposing classes that war is inevitable.

Democracy holds that free nations can settle differences justly and maintain a lasting peace.

These differences between communism and democracy do not concern the United States alone. People everywhere are coming to realize that what is involved is material well-being, human dignity, and the right to believe in and worship God.

I state these differences, not to draw issues of belief as such, but because the actions resulting from the Communist philosophy are a threat to the efforts of free nations to bring about world recovery and lasting peace.

Since the end of hostilities, the United States has invested its substance and its energy in a great constructive effort to restore peace, stability, and freedom to the world.

We have sought no territory. We have imposed our will on none. We have asked for no privileges we would not extend to others.

We have constantly and vigorously supported the United Nations and related agencies as a means of applying democratic principles to international relations. We have consistently advocated and relied upon peaceful settlement of disputes among nations.

We have made every effort to secure agreement on effective international control of our most powerful weapon, and we have worked steadily for the limitation and control of all armaments.

We have encouraged, by precept and example, the expansion of world trade on a sound and fair basis.

Almost a year ago, in company with 16 free nations of Europe, we launched the greatest cooperative program in history. The purpose of that unprecedented effort is to invigorate and strengthen democracy in Europe, so that the free people of that continent can resume their rightful place in the forefront of civilization and can contribute once more to the security and welfare of the world.

Our efforts have brought new hope to all mankind. We have beaten back despair and defeatism. We have saved a number of countries from losing their liberty. Hundreds of millions of people all over the world now agree with us, that we need not have war—that we can have peace.

The initiative is ours.

We are moving on with other nations to build an even stronger structure of international order and justice. We shall have as our partners countries which, no longer solely concerned with the problem of national survival, are now working to improve the standards of living of all their people. We are ready to undertake new projects to strengthen a free world.

In the coming years, our program for peace and freedom will emphasize four major courses of action.

First, we will continue to give unfaltering support to the United Nations and related agencies, and we will continue to search for ways to strengthen their authority and increase their effectiveness. We believe that the United Nations will be strengthened by the new nations which are being formed in lands now advancing toward self-government under democratic principles.

Second, we will continue our programs for world economic recovery.

This means, first of all, that we must keep our full weight behind the European recovery program. We are confident of the success of this major venture in world recovery. We believe that our partners in this effort will achieve the status of self-supporting nations once again.

In addition, we must carry out our plans for reducing the barriers to world trade and increasing its volume. Economic recovery and peace itself depend on increased world trade.

Third, we will strengthen freedom-loving nations against the dangers of aggression.

We are now working out with a number of countries a joint agreement designed to strengthen the security of the North Atlantic area. Such an agreement would take the form of a collective defense arrangement within the terms of the United Nations Charter.

We have already established such a defense pact for the Western Hemisphere by the Treaty of Rio de Janeiro.

The primary purpose of these agreements is to provide unmistakable proof of the joint determination of the free countries to resist armed attack from any quarter. Every country participating in these agreements must contribute all it can to the common defense.

If we can make it sufficiently clear, in advance, that any armed attack affecting our national security would be met with overwhelming force, the armed attack might never occur.

I hope soon to send to the Senate a treaty respecting the North Atlantic security plan.

In addition, we will provide military advice and equipment to free nations which will cooperate with us in the maintenance of peace and security.

Fourth, we must embark on a bold new program for making the benefits of our scientific advances and industrial progress available for the improvement and growth of underdeveloped areas.

More than half the people of the world are living in conditions approaching misery. Their food is inadequate. They are victims of disease. Their economic life is primitive and stagnant. Their poverty is a handicap and a threat both to them and to more prosperous areas.

For the first time in history, humanity possesses the knowledge and skill to relieve suffering of these people.

The United States is preeminent among the nations in the development of industrial and scientific techniques. The material resources which we can afford to use for assistance of other peoples are limited. But our imponderable resources in technical knowledge are constantly growing and are inexhaustible.

I believe that we should make available to peace-loving peoples the benefits of our store of technical knowledge in order to help them realize their aspirations for a better life. And, in cooperation with other nations, we should foster capital investment in areas needing development.

Our aim should be to help the free peoples of the world, through their own efforts, to produce more food, more clothing, more materials for housing, and more mechanical power to lighten their burdens,

We invite other countries to pool their technological resources in this undertaking. Their contributions will be warmly welcomed. This should be a cooperative enterprise in which all nations work together through the United Nations and its specialized agencies whenever practicable. It must be a worldwide effort for the achievement of peace, plenty, and freedom.

With the cooperation of business, private capital, agriculture, and labor in this country, this program can greatly increase the industrial activity in other nations and can raise substantially their standards of living.

Such new economic developments must be devised and controlled to the benefit of the peoples of the areas in which they are established. Guarantees to the investor must be balanced by guarantees in the interest of the people whose resources and whose labor go into these developments.

The old imperialism—exploitation for foreign profit—has no place in our plans. What we envisage is a program of development based on the concepts of democratic fair-dealing.

All countries, including our own, will greatly benefit from a constructive program for the better use of the world's human and natural resources. Experience shows that our commerce with other countries expands as they progress industrially and economically.

Greater production is the key to prosperity and peace. And the key to greater production is a wider and more vigorous application of modern scientific and technical knowledge.

Only by helping the least fortunate of its members to help themselves can the human family achieve the decent, satisfying life that is the right of all people.

Democracy alone can supply the vitalizing force to stir the peoples of the world into triumphant action, not only against their human oppressors, but also against their ancient enemies—hunger, misery, and despair.

On the basis of these four major courses of action we hope to create the conditions that will lead eventually to personal freedom and happiness for all mankind.

If we are to be successful in carrying out these policies, it is clear that we must have continued prosperity in this country and we must keep ourselves strong.

Slowly but surely we are weaving a world fabric of international security and growing prosperity.

We are aided by all who wish to live in freedom from fear—even by those who live today in fear under their own governments.

We are aided by all who want relief from lies and propaganda—those who desire truth and security.

We are aided by all who desire self-government and a voice in deciding their own affairs.

We are aided by all who long for economic security—for the security and abundance that men in free societies can enjoy.

We are aided by all who desire freedom of speech, freedom of religion, and freedom to live their own lives for useful ends.

Our allies are the millions who hunger and thirst after righteousness.

In due time, as our stability becomes manifest, as more and more nations come to know the benefits of democracy and to participate in growing abundance, I believe that those countries which now oppose us will abandon their delusions and join with the free nations of the world in a just settlement of international differences.

Events have brought our American democracy to new influence and new responsibilities. They will test our courage, our devotion to duty, and our concept of liberty.

But I say to all men, what we have achieved in liberty, we will surpass in greater liberty.

Steadfast in our faith in the Almighty, we will advance toward a world where man's freedom is secure.

To that end we will devote our strength, our resources, and our firmness of resolve. With God's help, the future of mankind will be assured in a world of justice, harmony, and peace.

Appeal to the League of Nations

From Ethiopian Emperor Haile Selassie
June, 1936, Geneva, Switzerland

I, Haile Selassie I, Emperor of Ethiopia, am here today to claim that justice which is due to my people, and the assistance promised to it eight months ago, when fifty nations asserted that aggression had been committed in violation of international treaties.

There is no precedent for a Head of State himself speaking in this assembly. But there is also no precedent for a people being victim of such injustice and being at present threatened by abandonment to its aggressor. Also, there has never before been an example of any Government proceeding to the systematic extermination of a nation by barbarous means, in violation of the most solemn promises made by the nations of the earth that there should not be used against innocent human beings the terrible poison of harmful gases. It is to defend a people struggling for its age-old independence that the head of the Ethiopian Empire has to come to Geneva to fulfill this supreme duty, after having himself fought at the head of his armies.

I pray to Almighty God that He may spare nations the terrible sufferings that have just been inflicted on my people, and of which the chiefs who accompany me here have been the horrified witnesses.

It is my duty to inform the Governments assembled here in Geneva, responsible as they are for the lives of millions of men, women and children, of the deadly peril which threatens them, by describing to them the fate which has been suffered by Ethiopia. It is not only upon the warriors that the Italian Government has made war. It has above all attacked populations far removed from hostilities, in order to exterminate them.

At the beginning, towards the end of 1935, Italian aircraft hurled upon my armies bombs of tear-gas. Their effects were but slight. The soldiers learned to scatter, waiting until the wind had rapidly dispersed the poisonous gases. The Italian aircraft then resorted to mustard gas.

Barrels of liquid were hurled upon armed groups. But this means also was not effective; the liquid affected only a few soldiers, and barrels upon the ground were themselves a warning to troops and the population of the danger.

It was at the time when operations for the encircling of Makalle were taking place that the Italian command, fearing a rout, followed procedure which it is now my duty to denounce to the world. Special sprayers were installed on board aircraft so that they could vaporize, over vast areas of territory, a fine, death-dealing rain. Groups of nine, fifteen, eighteen aircraft followed one another so that the fog issuing from them formed a continuous sheet. It was thus that, as from the end of January, 1936, soldiers, women, children, cattle, rivers, lakes and pastures were drenched continually with this deadly rain. In order to kill off systematically all living creatures, in order to more surely to poison waters and pastures, the Italian command made its aircraft pass over again and again. That was its chief method of warfare.

Ravage and Terror

The very refinement of barbarism consisted in carrying ravage and terror into the most densely populated parts of the territory, the points farthest removed from the scenes of hostilities. The object was to scatter fear and death over a great part of the Ethiopian territory. These fearful tactics succeeded. Men and animals succumbed. The deadly rain that fell from the aircraft made all those whom it touched fly shrieking with pain. All those who drank the poisoned water or ate the infected food also succumbed in dreadful suffering. In tens of thousands, the victims of the Italian mustard gas fell. It is in order to denounce to the civilized world the tortures inflicted upon the Ethiopian people that I resolved to come to Geneva. None other than myself and my brave companions in arms could bring the League of Nations the undeniable proof. The appeals of my delegates addressed to the League of Nations had remained without any answer; my delegates had not been witnesses. That is why I decided to come myself to bear witness against the crime perpetrated against my people and give Europe a warning of doom that awaits it, if it should bow before the accomplished fact.

Is it necessary to remind the Assembly of the various stages of the Ethiopian drama? For 20 years past, either as Heir Apparent, Regent of the Empire, or as Emperor, I have never ceased to use all my efforts to bring my country the benefits of civilization, and in particular to establish relations of good neighborliness with adjacent powers. In particular I succeeded in concluding with Italy the Treaty of Friendship of 1928, which absolutely prohibited the resort, under any pretext whatsoever, to force of arms, substituting for force and pressure the conciliation and arbitration on which civilized nations have based international order.

Country More United

In its report of October 5th, 1935, the Committee of Thirteen recognized my efforts and the results that I had achieved. The Governments thought that the entry of Ethiopia into the League, whilst giving that country a new guarantee for the maintenance of her territorial integrity and independence, would help her to reach a higher level of civilization. It does not seem that in Ethiopia today there is more disorder and insecurity than in 1923. On the contrary, the country is more united and central power is better obeyed.

I should have procured still greater results for my people if obstacles of every kind had not been put in the way by the Italian Government, the Government which stirred up revolt and armed the rebels. Indeed the Rome Government, as it has today openly proclaimed, has never ceased to prepare for the conquest of Ethiopia. The Treaties of Friendship it signed with me were not sincere; their only object was to hide its real intention from me. The Italian Government asserts that for 14 years it has been preparing for its present conquest. It therefore recognized today that when it supported the admission of Ethiopia to the League of Nations in 1923, when it concluded the Treaty of Friendship in 1928, when it signed the Pact of Paris outlawing war, it was deceiving the whole world. The Ethiopian Government was, in these solemn treaties, given additional guarantees of security which would enable it to achieve further progress along the specific path of reform on which it had set its feet, and to which it was devoting all its strength and all its heart.

Wal-Wal Pretext

The Wal-Wal incident, in December, 1934, came as a thunderbolt to me. The Italian provocation was obvious and I did not hesitate to appeal to the League of Nations. I invoked the provisions of the treaty of 1928, the principles of the Covenant; I urged the procedure of reconciliation and arbitration. Unhappily for Ethiopia this was the time when a certain Government considered that the European situation made it imperative at all costs to obtain the friendship of Italy. The price paid was the abandonment of Ethiopian independence to the greed of the Italian Government. This secret agreement, contrary to the obligations of the Covenant, has exerted a great influence over the course of events. Ethiopia and the whole world have suffered and are still suffering today its disastrous consequences.

This first violation of the Covenant was followed by many others. Feeling itself encouraged in its policy against Ethiopia, the Rome Government feverishly made war preparations, thinking that the concerted pressure which was beginning to be exerted on the Ethiopian Government, might perhaps not overcome the resistance of my people to Italian domination. The time had come, thus all sorts of difficulties were placed in the way with a view to breaking up the procedure; of conciliation and arbitration. All kinds of obstacles were placed in the way of that procedure. Governments tried to prevent the Ethiopian Government from finding arbitrators amongst the nationals: when once the arbitral tribunal was set up pressure was exercised so that an award favorable to Italy should be given.

All this was in vain: the arbitrators, two of whom were Italian officials, were forced to recognize unanimously that the Wal-Wal incident, as in the subsequent incidents, no international responsibility was to be attributed to Ethiopia.

Peace Efforts

Following on this award, the Ethiopian Government sincerely thought that an era of friendly relations might be opened with Italy. I loyally offered my hand to the Roman Government. The Assembly was informed by the report of the Committee of Thirteen, dated October 5th, 1935, of the details of the events which occurred after the month of December, 1934, and up to October 3rd, 1935.

It will be sufficient if I quote a few of the conclusions of that report Nos. 24, 25 and 26.

"The Italian memorandum (containing complaints made by Italy) was laid on the Council table on September 4th, 1935, whereas Ethiopia's first appeal to the Council had been made on December 14th, 1934. In the interval between those two dates, the Italian Government opposed the consideration of the question by the Council on the ground that the only appropriate procedure was that provided for in the Italo-Ethiopian Treaty of 1928. Throughout the whole of that period, moreover, the dispatch of Italian troops to East Africa was proceeding. These shipments of troops were represented to the Council by the Italian Government as necessary for the defense of its colonies menaced by Ethiopia's preparations. Ethiopia, on the contrary, drew attention to the official pronouncements made in Italy which, in its opinion, left no doubt as to the hostile intentions of the Italian Government."

From the outset of the dispute, the Ethiopian Government has sought settlement by peaceful means. It has appealed to the procedures of the Covenant. The Italian Government desiring to keep strictly to the procedures of the Italo-Ethiopian Treaty of 1928, the Ethiopian Government assented. It invariably stated that it would faithfully carry out the arbitral award even if the decision went against it. It agreed that the question of the ownership of Wal-Wal should not be dealt with by the arbitrators, because the Italian Government would not agree to such a course. It asked the Council to dispatch neutral observers and offered to lend itself to any enquiries upon which the Council might decide.

Once the Wal-Wal dispute had been settled by arbitration, however, the Italian Government submitted its detailed memorandum to the Council in support of its claim to liberty of action. It asserted that a case like that of Ethiopia cannot be settled by the means provided by the Covenant. It stated that, "since this question affects vital interest and is of primary importance to Italian security and civilization' it 'would be failing in its most elementary duty, did it not cease once for all to place any confidence in Ethiopia, reserving full liberty to adopt any measures that may become necessary to ensure the safety of its colonies and to safeguard its own interests."

Covenant Violated

Those are the terms of the report of the Committee of Thirteen, The Council and the Assembly unanimously adopted the conclusion that the Italian Government had violated the Covenant and was in a state of aggression. I did not hesitate to declare that I did not wish for war, that it was imposed upon me, and I should struggle solely for the independence and integrity of my people, and that in that struggle I was the defender of the cause of all small States exposed to the greed of a powerful neighbor.

In October, 1935, the 52 nations who are listening to me today gave me the assurance that the aggressor would not triumph, that the resources of the Covenant would be employed in order to ensure the reign of right and the failure of violence.

I ask the fifty-two nations not to forget today the policy upon which they embarked eight months ago, and on faith of which I directed the resistance of my people against the aggressor whom they denounced to the world. Despite the inferiority of my weapons, the complete lack of aircraft, artillery, munitions, hospital services, my confidence in the League was absolute. I thought it to be impossible that fifty-two nations, including the most powerful in the world, should be successfully opposed to a single aggressor. Counting on the faith due to treaties, I had made no preparations for war, and that is the case with certain small countries in Europe.

When the danger became more urgent, being aware of my responsibilities towards my people, during the first six months of 1935 I tried to acquire armaments. Many Governments proclaimed an embargo to prevent my doing so, whereas the Italian Government through the Suez Canal, was given all facilities for transporting without cessation and without protest, troops, arms, and munitions.

Forced to Mobilize

On October 3rd, 1935, the Italian troops invaded my territory. A few hours later only I decreed general mobilization. In my desire to maintain peace I had, following the example of a great country in Europe on the Eve of the Great War, caused my troops to withdraw thirty kilometers so as to remove any pretext of provocation.

War then took place in the atrocious conditions which I laid before the Assembly. In that unequal struggle between a Government commanding more than forty-two million inhabitants, having at its disposal financial, industrial and technical means which enabled it to create unlimited quantities of the most death-dealing weapons, and on the other hand, a small people of twelve million inhabitants, without arms, without resources having on its side only the justice of its own cause and the promise of the League of Nations. What real assistance was given to Ethiopia by the fifty-two who had declared the Rome Government guilty of a breach of the Covenant and had undertaken to prevent the triumph of the aggressor? Has each of the States members, as it was its duty to due in virtue of its signature appended to Article 15 of the Covenant, considered it the aggressor as having committed an act of war personally directed against itself? I had placed all my hopes in the execution of these undertakings. My confidence had been confirmed by the repeated declarations made in the Council to the effect that aggression must not be rewarded, and that force would end by being compelled to bow before right.

In December 15, 1935, the Council made it quite clear that its feelings were in harmony with those of hundreds of millions of people who, in all parts of the world, had protested against the proposal to dismember Ethiopia. It was constantly repeated that there was not merely a conflict between the Italian Government and the League of Nations, and that is why I personally refused all proposals to my advantage made to me by the Italian Government, if only I would betray my people and the Covenant of the League of Nations. I was defending the cause of small peoples who are threatened with aggression.

What of Promises?

What have become of the promises made to me as long ago as October, 1935? I noted with grief, but without surprise that the three Powers considered their undertakings under the Covenant as absolutely of no value. Their connections with Italy impelled them to refuse to take any measures whatsoever in order to stop Italian aggression. On the contrary, it was profound disappointment to me to learn the attitude of a certain Government, which, whilst ever protesting its scrupulous attachment to the Covenant, has tirelessly used all its efforts to prevent its observance. As soon as any measure which was likely to be rapidly effective was proposed, various pretexts were devised in order to postpone even consideration of the measure. Did the secret agreements of January, 1935, provide for this tireless obstruction?

The Ethiopian Government never expected other Governments to shed their soldiers' blood to defend the Covenant when their own immediately personal lands were not at stake. Ethiopian warriors asked only for means to defend themselves. On many occasions I have asked for financial assistance for the purchase of arms. That assistance has been constantly refused me. What, then, in practice, is the meaning of Article 16 of the Covenant and of collective security?

The Ethiopian Government's use of the railway from Djibouti to Addis Ababa was in practice a hazardous attempt in regards transport of arms intended for the Ethiopian forces. At the present moment this is the chief, if not the only means of supply to the Italian armies of occupation. The rules of neutrality should have prohibited transports intended for Italian forces, but there is not even neutrality since Article 16 lays upon every State Member of the League to duty not to remain a neutral but to come to the aid not of the aggressor but of the victim of aggression. Has the Covenant been respected? Is it today being respected?

Finally a statement has just been made in their Parliaments by the Governments of certain Powers, amongst them the most influential members of the League of Nations, that since the aggressor has succeeded in occupying a large part of Ethiopian territory they propose not to continue the application of any economic and financial measures that may have been decided upon against the Italian Government. These are the circumstances in which at the request of the Argentine Government, the Assembly of the League of Nations meets to consider the situation created by Italian aggression. I assert that the problem submitted to the Assembly today is a much wider one. It is not merely a question of the settlement of Italian aggression.

League Threatened

It is collective security: it is the very existence of the League of Nations. It is the confidence that each State is to place in international treaties. It is the value of promises made to small States that their integrity and their independence shall be respected and ensured. It is the principle of the equality of States on the one hand, or otherwise the obligation laid upon small Powers to accept the bonds of vassalship. In a word, it is international morality that is at stake. Have the signatures appended to a Treaty value only in so far as the signatory Powers have a personal, direct and immediate interest involved?

No subtlety can change the problem or shift the grounds of the discussion. It is in all sincerity that I submit these considerations to the Assembly. At a time when my people are threatened with extermination, when the support of the League may ward off the final blow, may I be allowed to speak with complete frankness, with out reticence, in all directness such as is demanded by the rule of equality as between all States Members of the League?

Apart from the Kingdom of the Lord there is not on this earth any nation that is superior to any other. Should it happen that a strong Government finds it may with impunity destroy a weak people, then the hour strikes for that weak people to appeal to the League of Nations to give its judgment in all freedom. God and history will remember your judgment.

Assistance Refused

I have heard it asserted that the inadequate sanctions already applied have not achieved their object. At no time, and under no circumstances could sanctions that were intentionally badly applied, stop an aggressor. This not a case of the impossibility of stopping an aggressor but of the refusal to stop an aggressor. When Ethiopia requested and requests that she should be given financial assistance, was that a measure which it was impossible to apply whereas financial assistance of the League has been granted, even in times of peace, to two countries and exactly two countries who have refused to apply sanctions against the aggressor?

Faced by numerous violations by the Italian Government of all international treaties that prohibit resort to arms, and the use of barbarous methods of warfare, it is my painful duty to note that the initiative has today been taken with a view of raising sanctions. Does this initiative not mean in practice the abandonment of Ethiopia to the aggressor? On the very eve of the day when I was about to attempt a supreme effort in the defense of my people before this Assembly does not this initiative deprive Ethiopia of one of her last chances to succeed in obtaining the support and guarantee of State Members? Is that the guidance the League of Nations and each of the State Members are entitled to expect from the great Powers when they assert their right and their duty to guide the action of the League? Placed by the aggressor face to face with the accomplished fact, are States going to set up terrible precedent of bowing before force?

Your Assembly will doubtless have laid before it proposals for the reform of the Covenant and for rendering more effective the guarantee of collective security. Is it the Covenant that needs reform? What undertakings can have any value if the will to keep them is lacking? It is international morality which is at stake and not the Articles of Covenant. On behalf of the Ethiopian people, a member of the League of Nations, I request the Assembly to take all measures proper to ensure respect for the Covenant. I renew my protest against the violations of treaties of which the Ethiopian people has been the victim. I declare in the face of the whole world that the Emperor, the Government and the people of Ethiopia will not bow before force; that they maintain their claim that they will use all means in their power to ensure triumph of right and the respect for the Covenant.

I ask the fifty-two nations, who have given the Ethiopian people a promise to help them in their resistance to the aggressor, what are they willing to do for Ethiopia? And the great Powers who have promised the guarantee of collective security to small States on whom weighs the threat that they may one day suffer the fate of Ethiopia, I ask what measures do you intend to take?

Representatives of the World I have come to Geneva to discharge in your midst the most painful of the duties of the head of a State. What reply shall I have to take back to my People?

Letter of Benjamin H. Hardy to Mr. Jonathan Daniels, Raleigh, North Carolina

November 19, 1950

Dear Mr. Daniels,

    In response to your request of Nov. 2, I will be glad to tell you what I know of the origins of Point Four. However, I feel that I must ask you to observe certain conditions concerning the use of the information. I do not want to appear hypocritical, as I appreciate recognition as much as most people do. But I have not sought public credit for my part in the conception of Point Four, out of deference to the President and because I consider the idea itself more important than how it came about. I think it would be unwise for the full story I relate below not to be told until after the Point Four program is much more firmly established than it now is, since the very manner in which it the initial proposal originated would be used by hostile critics to attack it and the President. It is for this reason that I ask that the full story not be revealed until the telling of it will no longer jeopardize the future of the program. I also ask that my memorandum not be published or quoted from without my permission.

    For me, I suppose Point Four began when I was in Brazil in 1944-46 as press officer for the Office of the Coordinator of Inter-American Affairs, and saw at first hand some of the work being done there in technical assistance projects, and also the great opportunities and needs for this kind of aid. I returned home with greater appreciation, gained from the vantage point of a relatively underdeveloped country, of how the immense moral and material power might be used for the benefit of ourselves and others. I also returned with a desire personally to do more for the world, if possible, than simply fertilize it with my bones. At that time, however, I had no clear-cut conception of what was to become known as Point Four. In February 1947 I was employed as a writer in the Office of Public Affairs in the Department of State, and soon came to specialize in speech writing, as part of my job. I drafted some speeches for Secretary Marshall while the Marshall Plan was under public consideration (but not the Harvard speech).

In the fall of 1948 I began to wonder what new move the U. S. could make in the "cold war" which would enable us to capitalize upon the advantages gained through launching the Marshall Plan, and to retain the initiative and make further gains in winning world opinion to our side. I also felt that more could be done in a positive way to ameliorate the misery and despair in which much of the world was living. It was then that I remembered what I had learned in Brazil, and it occurred to me that a massive, world-wide technical assistance program was at least a large part of the answer.

Accordingly, in November I wrote a memorandum outlining this proposal and sent it to my superior, Francis H. Russell, Director of the Office of Public Affairs. He called two meetings of State Department officials to consider the suggestion, the first comprising about half a dozen people and the second about 12 or 15. At this second meeting, strong opposition was expressed on the grounds that the Budget Bureau had just cut back the request for funds for the SCC program for the fiscal year 1950 and that a proposal for a large-scale program of the same kind would be "suicidal."

Just before the second meeting took place, Clark Clifford sounded out acting secretary Lovett (Marshall was then in the hospital) on the possibility of developing the President's inaugural address as a major foreign policy statement—a kind of "democratic manifesto." The request came down "through channels" and I was directed to prepare a draft. I discussed the assignment with Francis Russell and proposed that we include in the draft at least the embryo of the technical assistance idea, and he agreed. About this time I revised my original memorandum slightly and incorporated the suggestion that the proposal be included in the President's inaugural address as the "punch line." I am enclosing a copy of this version of the memorandum, which you note was dated December 15, 1948.

About the same time, I completed my draft of the proposed inaugural address, which included a rather brief statement advocating that the U. S. embark on a technical assistance program. This draft went up "through channels" and I learned a few days later that it had been almost completely rewritten, with the technical assistance section deleted, and the new draft had been sent to the White House. Francis Russell also told me that he had shown my memorandum to Mr. Lovett, who after reading it expressed the opinion that this was not the kind of thing the President was looking for.

At this point I was more convinced than ever that the idea for a technical assistance program was sound and would constitute a powerful weapon for democracy in the struggle against communism, and I determined to do what I could to see that it at least got a hearing on its merits. Therefore I telephoned George Elsey, whom I had not met but with whom I had talked by telephone on previous assignments, and arranged to see him. I related what had taken place and left with him a copy of my Dec. 15 memo.

Either the last week in December or the first week in January, Francis Russell told me that the White House had informed the State Department that the draft inaugural address it had submitted was not satisfactory. He instructed me to prepare another draft. He and Clark Clifford talked by phone about the content of the speech, and agreed that it should contain what later appeared as four points. Francis, of course, was familiar with my memo and, although I have never met or talked with Clark Clifford, I feel sure that he had received a copy from George Elsey. (At that time, I had told no one of my contact with Elsey.)

I took my original draft of the speech, tightened it up and further refined it, and expanded the section on technical assistance. The time was then about a week before inauguration day. The draft went to the White House, where it underwent further revision, and a copy was referred to the State Department for comment only about 48 hours before it was to be delivered. It was changed only slightly as a result of these comments, and delivered in that form by the President.

As you will note from a comparison of my memorandum with the text of the inaugural address, the idea underwent some changes at the White House. The major change was that my proposal embraced only technical assistance; although I realized in a general way that capital investment also was necessary. I assumed it would come largely from the World Bank, the Export-Import Bank and similar sources; I certainly did not give capital investment the emphasis it received in the speech as delivered. Also, I was thinking in terms of a worldwide technical assistance program, which in the industrialized countries of Western Europe would be directed toward modernization and more efficient production—something which the ECS has been emphasizing in the latter phase of ERP. I had no thought of singling out the underdeveloped areas as the exclusive focus of the program, although, as my memo indicates, it was obvious that these areas offered the greatest opportunities for utilizing the simpler and less expensive techniques. Moreover, I did not designate the four "points" in the speech as such or label technical assistance "a bold, new program."

These are the essential facts as I know them. While I do not intend to seek any personal advantage from my part in the genesis of Point Four, I am proud of the contribution I was able to make, not only in formulating the Point Four concept, but also in framing and drafting much of the language used in the inaugural address, which I think admirably served the purposes for which it was intended and, potentially at least, did have the impact of a "democratic manifesto."

My great concern is that this potentially invaluable asset has not been adequately exploited. The Point Four program which has emerged after much delay falls short of the great promise that the President's inaugural pronouncement contained, and which was widely recognized and acclaimed at the time. It may be that with the continued strong support of the President and others who believe in the Point Four concept as devotedly as he does, the effort can gain momentum and yet achieve its purpose. But the election returns appear to me to be ominous for the future of Point Four, despite the merits which in my opinion should appeal to almost all shades of political opinion.

As you may know, I am now Public Affairs Officer in the Technical Cooperation Administration, set up by the State Department to handle the Point Four program. I took this job in order to continue to do what I can to make the program a success. I have been most favorably impressed by the common sense, humanitarian sensibilities, and political acumen of your fellow North Carolinian, Ambassador Waynick, as Acting Administrator. I regret that he will not continue to direct our operations in the critical days ahead.

If Point Four is to achieve the great purposes for which it was designed, it must do so as the result of the misunderstanding, effort and support of the informed and progressive elements of our country. I trust that you, Mr. Daniels, will continually exert your efforts and influence, both personally and through your paper, in behalf of a cause which I believe is worthy of the best effort of all of us.

Sincerely yours, Benjamin H. Hardy.

Remarks Recorded by Mr. James E. Webb, Under-Secretary of State, January 7, 1952, Regarding the death of Dr. Henry Garland Bennett

Today a great and loyal son of Oklahoma has come home. Since he left this State, which he loved so dearly, Dr. Henry Bennett has become known and revered by men and women all over the world. In the last year he had talked, as a neighbor and a friend to men in Asia, in Africa, in South America.

Yet it seemed that Dr. Bennett's ties with Oklahoma became, if possible, stronger. His strength came from her soil. His vision was as wide as her horizons. From the history of her early days and from his own youth grew his unshakable belief in the dignity of work. In particular, he valued the man who works on the land.

I know these things because in the past year we worked together in a close day-to-day relationship. I watched the Point 4 Program grow under his guidance. At the time of his death, it was beginning to bear fruit in many lands. I am convinced that this growth was possible because Dr. Bennett was driven by a single passion—he loved his fellow man. This love was wise, understanding, and above all practical.

It was wise in that he saw the innate capacities in all human beings. It was understanding in his respect for other men's beliefs and aspirations. That his love was eminently practical is best expressed in these words from the Talmud, which he himself was fond of quoting: "The noblest charity is to prevent a man from accepting charity; and the best alms are to show and to enable a man to dispense with alms."

But love alone could not have done what Dr. Bennett accomplished. In addition, he had great ability, driving energy, and the gift of leadership.

You who were his neighbors and friends in Oklahoma, do not mourn alone. We, his associates in the State Department, miss his guidance and his warmth more each day. Still others in many lands have sent expressions of sympathy and esteem.

Because of his whole-hearted devotion to a great idea, men and women who knew only the struggle against poverty, disease, and despair, now know hope. They can see the vision of a new world for their children. That is Dr. Bennett's greatest memorial. It will be the duty and the privilege of all who revered this great leader to carry his work forward in his spirit of love and service to our fellow men.

Draft Speech for Acting Secretary James E. Webb at the University of North Carolina

Written by Benjamin Hardy, U. S. State Department
Delivered June 3, 1949

I am deeply grateful that the university which awarded me the Bachelor of Arts degree 21 years ago considers me worthy to be the recipient today of the honorary degree of Doctor of Laws. Recognition by those who know us best touches us most deeply, and I especially cherish this honor from the University of North Carolina.

Naturally my thoughts turn to that other commencement day in 1928 and the many profound changes that have taken place in the intervening years. It is a truism that the world changes, that the human society of which we are a part is never static but lives and moves and has a being of its own. But such truths sometimes are in danger of losing their meaning through being taken too much for granted. We must continually examine them anew if we are really to understand their meaning and be guided by them.

One of the greatest changes that has occurred in this period is that you and I are no longer citizens of a nation that is merely one among many. We are citizens of the nation to which the free people of the world look for leadership and security. This turn of history places on the United States a tremendous responsibility, which all of its citizens share and will continue to share for many years.

Our first duty is to realize that the role of leadership which has devolved upon our country is one that cannot be put on or taken off at will, like a garment to suit the occasion. We must recognize the nature and extent of our responsibilities and be prepared to carry them indefinitely into the future, if we are not to default in the great task that is ours. We must comprehend that we can never act, as we sometimes have thought we could act in the past, without regard to the consequences to the rest of the world. We must not only be purposeful and resolute, we must so conduct ourselves that others will never doubt our purpose and our resolution. Our every act is fraught with meaning for the people of the world and they are mindful of the fact.

Mr. Henry L. Stimson, who served his country both as Secretary of State and Secretary of War, has summed up the consequences to us in this way, "No private program and no public policy, in any sector of our national life, can now escape from the compelling fact that if it is not framed with reference to the world, it is framed with perfect futility."

What does this mean in practical terms? It means that the borderline between domestic and foreign affairs has practically ceased to exist. It means that we must so organize and so conduct our affairs that we are not only able to discharge the enormous responsibilities of world leadership, but that we can do so with increasing success. It means that our government must be made a more efficient and more effective instrument for executing the will of the American people and attaining the ends they seek.

This is the significance of the great amount of work and the considerable amount of discussion concerning government reorganization you have been hearing about from Washington. It is far from an academic matter. It is a very practical and realistic consideration that vitally affects the course of our country in both domestic and foreign affairs.

I am glad to be able to report that the Department of State is rather far advanced in its program of reorganization along the lines laid down by the Hoover Commission. Many of the Commission's recommendations were, in fact, based on plans drawn in the Department.

We also have the very great advantage that Secretary Acheson served as vice chairman of the Hoover Commission and was thoroughly prepared to put the majority of the recommendations into effect almost immediately. The Congress quickly enacted legislation authorizing the appointment of additional assistant secretaries and they have now been nominated. When they take office, a clear line of authority will be in effect throughout the Department and the Secretary will be relieved of a great deal of detail. He will be able to devote his attention almost entirely to major policy matters. The Foreign Service, which the United States abroad, will be more closely coordinated with the work of the Department personnel in Washington.

But efficiency in the State Department will not of itself insure the success of our foreign policy. As the Hoover Commission pointed out, "Of 59 major departments and agencies in the executive branch, at least 46 are drawn into foreign affairs to a greater or lesser extent." This is one index of the complexity of foreign policy in these times, especially the foreign policy of a democracy.

And not only must the interest and activities of the agencies of the executive branch be coordinated and harmonized. The part played by the Congress in foreign affairs has become significantly greater, and teamwork between the executive and the legislative branches is therefore vitally important.

Public opinion also plays a major part in the foreign policy of a democracy. In the final analysis, public opinion is decisive because in our democratic system no policy that is not understood and supported by the American people can be successfully maintained. I should like to observe here that I think our colleges and universities can find a rich field for constructive endeavor in the stimulation of greater public understanding of and participation in foreign affairs. This observation is particularly pertinent at this University, which for many years has been an intellectual and cultural center of a whole region and which very recently released its distinguished president, Dr. Frank Graham, to enable him to take a larger part in national affairs as a member of the United States Senate.

The Senate now has before it, for its advice and consent to ratification, more than thirty international instruments which affect the foreign policy of the United States. Some are more important and urgent than others, but the variety and the scope of the legislation now pending underscore the extent of this nation's participation in world affairs.

It is essential that we do not permit the significance or the urgency of a particular measure at a given time to obscure the interrelationship of the various elements of our foreign policy. They are interdependent parts of the whole, each having an essential purpose. We may with good reason sometimes emphasize one aspect more than others, but in the long run we must keep the various factors in balance and move forward along a broad front.

Only a few months ago the serious weakness of the European economy as a result of the war had brought Western Europe to the verge of economic collapse, with attendant political dangers of the gravest kind. Prompt and effective cooperative action by the United States and the free nations of Europe, in the forms of the European Recovery program, turned the tide and Western Europe was transformed from a danger spot to a strong center of democracy.

Yet this gain will be temporary if we do not take further measures to capitalize on the success achieved thus far. Even with the momentum gained by the Marshall Plan, Western Europe can hope to become self-supporting and self-reliant after 1952 only in a healthy world economy characterized by vigorous and expanding world trade. Such an economic environment favorable to freedom and democracy can best be assured by a liberal and constructive trade policy on the part of the United States, made manifest through the continuance of the Reciprocal Trade Agreements program and ratification of the Charter of the International Trade Organization.

Conversely, a forward-looking economic foreign policy can be fully successful only in a peaceful and stable political environment. The political counterpart of the Marshall Plan is the North Atlantic Treaty, which unites the free nations on both sides of the Atlantic in a common defense against the threat of aggression. The chief immediate value of the Treaty is that it gives the nations of Western Europe the sense of security against the armed attacks which they require in order to devote their full energy to the task of economic recovery. The Treaty has now been before the nation more than two months and has won the overwhelming support of public opinion, which has been reflected in the hearings before the Senate Committee on Foreign Relations.

The companion legislation, providing American military assistance to the free nations to the extent of one billion, 450 million dollars in the next fiscal year, is an essential element in the over-all program for strengthening the democratic world. The bulk of this military assistance, or approximately one billion, 130 million dollars worth, would go to the European members of the North Atlantic Treaty. The reason for this is that almost without exception, the nations of western Europe came out of the war practically defenseless and have been able to make only a beginning in restoring their military strength. In order to encourage and enable them to make their proper contributions to the mutual defense potential under the North Atlantic Treaty, the United States can further its own interest by assisting its European partners to recover their military strength on the principle of self-help and mutual aid that has worked so well in the European Recovery Program.

Once the North Atlantic Treaty is in operation, this government should be in position to begin at once to supply the military assistance to make the Treaty fully effective. It is a matter of urgent necessity that the military assistance program be enacted into law during the present session of Congress. It is an essential element in the policy which the United States is pursuing in foreign affairs with increasing promise of success.

Hesitancy or delay in this matter would only hearten the enemies of democracy and weaken the confidence of the free peoples in the leadership of the United States which has brought the world thus far along the road to recovery and peace. We can't march up the hill one day, and then march down again the next. We must go forward, step, by step, to world peace and security. For only in such a world can our own peace and security be assured.

Photos

Photos sources are from the Bennett family; William Holloway, Jr.; Oklahoma History Center; Kerr Museum; Truman Presidential Library; and Benjamin Hardy, III.

Bennett family circa 1893, (L to R) Mary Elizabeth, Stella, Lois, Henry and Thomas Jefferson

Oklahoma A & M President Bennett presenting his "Twenty-five Year Plan" for the campus

Bennett family, Oklahoma A&M, 1949, Stillwater, Oklahoma

Bennett family reunion at Ouachita Baptist University, Arkadelphia, Arkansas, March 2, 2007, commemorating the 100th anniversary of Henry Bennett's college graduation

Bennetts'/Hardy crash site marker, Teheran, Iran, 1952

Dr. & Mrs. Bennett Memorial Service program cover, January, 1952

In Memoriam
Dr. and Mrs. Henry G. Bennett

Left: Bennett statue, Oklahoma State University campus, 1991, Stillwater, Oklahoma

Below: Tom Edwin Bennett and author at Oklahoma History Center Bennett exhibit unveiling, Oklahoma City, Oklahoma

1912 Hugo High School annual page showing Bennett as superintendent and William Holloway as teacher

The author with Judge William Holloway, Jr., at his office in Oklahoma City, Oklahoma

Oklahoma Governor William Judson Holloway official photo

Above: Kerr family Oklahoma homestead

Right: 1944 Kerr campaign poster

*Above:
President
Kennedy and
Senator Kerr at
an Oklahoma
project
dedication*

*Left: Senator
Robert Kerr
official photo
inscribed to
William
Holloway*

Above: President Truman delivering his 1949 Inauguration Speech

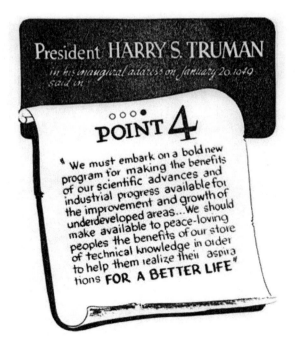

President HARRY S. TRUMAN

in his inaugural address on January 20, 1949 said in

○ ○ ○ ●

POINT 4

" We must embark on a bold new program for making the benefits of our scientific advances and industrial progress available for the improvement and growth of underdeveloped areas...We should make available to peace-loving peoples the benefits of our store of technical knowledge in order to help them realize their aspirations **FOR A BETTER LIFE**"

President Harry Truman, Assistant Secretary of State James Webb and Henry Bennett

James Webb, President Truman and Secretary of State Dean Acheson

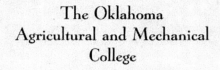

The Oklahoma
Agricultural and Mechanical
College

Reception

In honour of

His Imperial Majesty

Haile Selassie I

Emperor of Ethiopia

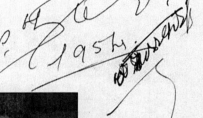

June 18, 1954

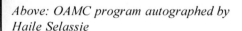

*Above: OAMC program autographed by
Haile Selassie*

*Left: His Royal Highness, Ethiopian
Emperor Haile Selassie*

*Left: Oklahoma A & M
President Bennett and
Ethiopian Emperor
Haile Selaissie, 1950*

*Below: Selaissie and
Bennett family Selaissie
and Oklahoma State
University*

Christine and Benjamin Hardy

This is one of the last pictures made of Dr. and Mrs. Bennett and A. Cyril Crilley and Benjamin Hardy. This picture may have been made in Jerusalem since they visited there before leaving Baghdad. Crilley, left; Hardy, right.

Above: Last known photograph of A Cyril Crilley, Dr. and Mrs. Bennett and Benjamin Hardy in Bethlehem before their untimely deaths, December, 1951

Left: Benjamin Hardy, Jr. at the U. S. State Department office

Senator Robert Kerr and James Webb at a NASA testing site

President John F. Kennedy and new NASA Director James Webb

President John F. Kennedy and NASA Director James Webb during a NASA visit, November, 1963

NASA Director James Webb and President Lyndon B. Johnson in the White House Oval Office

Bennett Family

Solomon Bennett (c1756)
  Ethelred Bennett (1780)
    Richard Allen Bennett (1801)
      George Washington Bennett (1828)
        Thomas Jefferson Bennett (1855)
          Henry Garland Bennett (1886)

Henry Garland Bennett, Jr.
  Jacque Bennett Holmes
    Elizabeth Drake
    Helen Connell Pinckney, III
  Nancy Bennett Noxon
    Julie Holland
    Kimberly Witter
    Robyn Marrs

Phil Connell Bennett
  Henry Garland Bennett, III
    Phil Bennett, II
    Suzanne Lynn Bennett Huck
    Richard Craig Bennett
    Kathryn Alexis Bennett Clark
    Corbin Bennett
  Lela Bennett Sullivan
    Connell Sullivan Branan, IV
      Clifford Branan, V
      Langley Bennett Branan
    Carla Stover Sullivan, Jr.
  Corabell Bennett Arps
    Elizabeth Arps Seymour
      Audrey Seymour
      Joseph Conner Seymour
    Joseph Warren Arps

Liberty Loven Bennett Preston
Vera Alma Preston-Jaeger
Melissa Rainwater
Mark Callahan
Patricia Preston
Ami Reed
Michelle Polk
Sophie Parrot
Trula Preston Dougherty
Chad Dougherty
Josh Dougherty
Libby Preston Bethel
Ryan Brown
Jenny Brown

Mary Lois Bennett DeLozier
Mac DeLozier
Tom DeLozier
Mac DeLozier, Jr.
Patrick DeLozier
Marlissa DeLozier
Phil DeLozier
Megan DeLozier
Barbara DeLozier
Elizabeth DeLozier
Henry Bennett DeLozier
Tom DeLozier
Vera Lou Walmsley
Mary Harris, Jr.

Thomas Edwin Bennett
Beverly Bennett Groom
Caroline Elizabeth Groom
Elizabeth Bennett
David Bennett
Matthew James Bennett
Tom Bennett, Jr.
Thomas Edwin Bennett, III
Tom E. Bennett, IV
James D. Bennett
Henry Garland Bennett, IV

Resources

Books

Arrington, Michael. *Ouachita Baptist University, The First 100 Years*. Little Rock, Arkansas: August House, 1985.

Arrington, Michael, and Downs, Bill. *Once in a Hundred Years*. Marceline, Missouri, 1985.

Bass, Paul. *The History of Debate at Ouachita Baptist University, 1886 to Present*. Arkadelphia, Arkansas: Campus Activities Office, 2002.

Bass, Paul. *No Little Dreams*. Stillwater, Oklahoma: Cimarron River Press, 2007.

Beisner, Robert L. *Dean Acheson, a Life in the Cold War*. New York: Oxford University Press, 2006

Boggs, James H. *Governance, Centennial Histories Series*. Stillwater, Oklahoma: Oklahoma State University, 1992.

Bourgoin, Suzanne Michele, and Byers, Paula Kay. *Encyclopedia of World Biography*. Detroit, Michigan: Gale Research, 1998. pages 68-70.

Candee, Marjorie Dent. *Current Biography 1954*. New York City, New York: H. W. Wilson Company, 1954. pages 315-317.

Chappell, Craig. *Research, Centennial Histories Series*. Stillwater, Oklahoma: Oklahoma State University, 1991.

Chronicles of Oklahoma, Volume 33, Oklahoma History Center, Oklahoma City, Oklahoma.

Clifford, Clark. *Counsel to the President*. Garden City, New York: Doubleday & Company, Inc., 1991.

Current Biography, "Haile Selassie," 1954.

Elsey, George McKee. *An Unplanned Life*. Columbia, Missouri: University of Missouri Press, 2005.

Encyclopedia of World Biography, Volume 7, "Haile Selassie"

Ferrell, Robert H. *Dear Bess, The Letters from Harry to Bess Truman 1910-1959*. New York: W. W. Norton & Company, 1983.

Ferrell, Robert H. *Off the Record, The Private Papers of Harry S. Truman*. New York, New York: Harper & Row, 1980.

Ferrell, Robert H. *Truman, A Century of Remembrance*. New York: Viking Press, 1984

Fischer, LeRoy. *Oklahoma's Governors, 1929-1955*. Oklahoma Historical Society, Oklahoma City, Oklahoma, 1983.

Fite, Robert C. *Extension and Outreach, Centennial Histories Series*. Stillwater, Oklahoma: Oklahoma State University, 1988.

Garraty, John A., and Carnes, Mark C. *American National Biography, Volume 22*. New York City, New York: Oxford University Press, 1999. pages 848-850.

Garraty, John A., and Carnes, Mark C. *American National Biography, Volume 12*. New York City, New York: Oxford University Press, 1999. pages 628-629.

Gill, Jerry L. *International Programs, Centennial Histories Series*. Oklahoma State University, Stillwater, Oklahoma, 1991.

Harlow, Rex. *Makers of Government in Oklahoma*. (old manuscript in Oklahoma Historical Society Research Center, Oklahoma City, Oklahoma)

Hechler, Ken. *Working with Truman*. New York: G. P. Putnam's Sons, 1982.

Kings and Queens, "Haile Selassie," Lambright, W. Henry, *Powering Apollo*, Baltimore: John Hopkins University Press, 1995

Marcus, Harold G. *Haile Selassie I: The Formative Years, 1892-1936*. Los Angeles: UC Press, 1987

Marshall Cavendish Benchmark. *Cultures of the World, Ethiopia*. Tarrytown, New York, 1996. pages 22-25.

McCullough, David. *Truman*. New York, New York: Simon & Schuster, 1992

McMillan Library Reference USA. *Kings & Queens*. New York: McMillan, 1999. pages 157-159.

Norris, L. David. *A History of Southeastern Oklahoma State University Since 1909, Volume 1*. Durant, Oklahoma: Mesa Publishing Company, 1986.

Noyes, David, and Flynn, Edward J. *The Buck Stops Here*. New York City, New York: Writers Club Press, 2000.

Pakenham, Thomas. *The Scramble for Africa*. New York City, New York: Avon Books, 1991. page 673.

Piers, Bizony, *The Man Who Ran the Moon*, New York: Thunder's Mouth Press, 2006

Poen, Monte M. *Letters Home By Harry Truman*. New York, G. P Putnam's Sons, 1984.

Rulon, Philip Reed. *Oklahoma State University—Since 1890*. Stillwater, Oklahoma, 1975.

Tareke, Gebru. *Ethiopia: Power and Protest*. Cambridge UP

Thoburn, Joseph B. and Wright, Muriel H. *Oklahoma, A History of Its State and Its People*. (old manuscript in Oklahoma Historical Society Research Center, Oklahoma City, Oklahoma), 1929.

Trouty, Chris, and Eugene Rosenfield. *Historical Dictionary of Ethiopia*, London: The Scarecrow Press, 1982

Truman, Harry S. *Memoirs, Volume Two*. Garden City, New York: Doubleday & Company, Inc., 1956.

Williams, Fay, and Allards, C. C. *Arkansans of the Years*, 1952.

Articles

"Plows and Sacred Cows," *Time*, January 22, 1951.

"Point Four," *War on Hunger*, May, 1973.

"Point IV: Early Trials," *War on Hunger*, October, 1973

"The Most Important Job," *War on Hunger*, November, 1973

"Point IV: Alive and Well," *War on Hunger*, January, 1974

Speech Release, USAID, January 20, 1999

American Experience, The Presidents, Harry S. Truman, PBS series

The Bureaucrat, Professional Leaders Series, "James E. Webb and NASA," Summer, 1986 and Fall, 1986

The Gannetteer, "James E. Webb: Space Age's Incredible Leader," October, 1974

Wall Street Journal, ""NASA's Jim Webb— a Rare Bureaucrat," October 11, 1968

Web Sites

(www.flyingfarmers.org/history)

(www.factmonster.com/ce6/history/A0839466)

(www.odur.let.rug.nl/~usa/P/ht33/truman)

(www.esuhistoryprof.com/truman/topics)

(www.essayexpress.com/essay/018270)

(www.tampa.craiglist.org/clt/76334080)

(www.rootsweb.com/~oknowata/holloway)

(www.geocities.com/lakehamiltom.ar/)

(www.http://libinfo.uark/specialcollections/manuscripts/Sizerguide,asp)

(www.itd.nps.gov/cwss/soldiers)

(www.alemayau.edu.et/pages/aboutus.html)

(www.farmhouse.org/may_why_I_give.html)

(www.okhighered.org/gold-book/part2.shtml)

(www.acutri@sandiego.edu)

(www.boomshaka/league.html)

(www.cnn.com) 2001, "Ethiopian Emperor Haile Selaissie finds final resting place"

(www.ieo.okstate.edu)

(www.pbs.org/AmericanExperience)

(www.worldwarI.com/tgws)

(www.jwst.nasa.gov)

Research Trips

Choctaw County Courthouse, Hugo, Oklahoma, July, 2005, fourth floor record archives, ledger of Choctaw County Teacher Employments

Southeastern Oklahoma State University, Durant, Oklahoma, July, 2005, Bennett Memorial Library archives

Highland Cemetery, Durant, Oklahoma, July, 2005, Bennett family graves

Oklahoma State University, Stillwater, Oklahoma, July, 2005, Edmon Law Library archives, Bennett statue

Oklahoma History Center, Oklahoma City, Oklahoma, numerous trips, 2006-2007, Bennett files, Bennett speech recording

Tulsa and Oklahoma City, Oklahoma, April 30 – May 2, 2007. Tom Bennett. Jr., Richard Poole and Frances Bennett

Bengin-Ozan Cemetery, Nashville, Arkansas

Nevada County Courthouse, Prescott, Arkansas

Clark County Courthouse, Arkadelphia, Arkansas

Mt. Moriah Church and Cemetery, Mt. Moriah, Arkansas

Southwest Arkansas Regional Historical Archives, Old Washington, Arkansas, July 13, 2007

Oklahoma City, Oklahoma, August 23, 2007, Judge William Holloway, Jr., Federal Courthouse Building.

Garland County Public Library, September 8, 2007, Hot Springs, Arkansas.

Truman Presidential Library Archives, September 26, 2007, Independence, Missouri

> Henry Bennett files

> Benjamin Hardy files

> Oral Interviews Transcripts:

>> **Bennett family** (Liberty Loven [Bennett] Preston, Mary Lois [Bennett] Delozier and Mary B. [Delozier] Harris), Stillwater, Oklahoma, 1971

>> **Dean Acheson**, Secretary of State, 1949-1953 (Washington, D. C., June 30, 1971

>> **Stanley Andrews**, Department of Agriculture, 1947-1951; Director of Technical Cooperation Administration (Point Four program), 1952-1953 (October 31, 1970)

>> **Leland Barrows**, Executive Assistant to the Special Representatives in Europe, Economic Cooperation Administration, 1948-1953 (Washington, D. C., January 8, 1971)

>> **Merwin L. Bohan**, U. S. Ambassador to the Inter-American Economic and Social Council, 1951-1955 (Dallas, Texas, June 15, 1974)

>> **Clark M. Clifford**, Special Counsel to the President, 1946-1950 (March 23, 1971/ October 4, 1073)

>> **Douglas Ensminger**, U. S. Department of Agriculture, 1939-1951 (Columbia, Missouri, June 16/ July 7, 1976)

Lincoln Gordon, Special Assistant to the President, 1050-1951 (Washington, D. C., July17/22, 1975)

Samuel P. Hayes, Foreign Economic Administration and U. S. State Department, 1942-1953 (July 16, 1975)

Henry Van Zile Hyde, U. S. Representative, World Health Organization, 1948-1952 (Bethesda, Maryland, July 24, 1975)

Christine Hardy Little, wife of Benjamin Hardy (Arlington, Virginia, February 23, 1973)

Dr. Raymond W. Miller, Consultant to the Food and Agricultural Organization of the United Nations, 1949-1953, and consultant for the Point Four program, 1949-1956 (Washington, D. C., October 13, 1969)

Hoyt E. Walkup and Russell L. Babb (Henry Bennett's pilots) (Stillwater, Oklahoma, March 17, 1971)

Francis Russell, Director, Office of Public Affairs, U. S. Department of State, 1945-1952 (Turner, Maine, July 13, 1976)

William E. Warne, Assistant Secretary, Department of Interior, 1947-1951; U. S. Minister in Charge of Technical Cooperation Administration (Point Four program), Iran, 1951-1955 (Independence, Missouri, May 21, 1988)

C. Tyler Wood, Assistant Administrator for Operations, 1949-1950; Deputy U. S. Representative in Europe, 1950-1952 (Washington, D. C. June 18, 1971)

Interviews

Bennett Family:
> David Bennett
> Elizabeth Bennett
> Frances Bennett
> Thomas Edwin Bennett
> Tom Bennett, Jr.
> Raymond Bright
> Norene Bryant
> Roxi Lawrence
> Nancy Noxon
> Tricia Preston
> Vera Preston-Jaeger
> Lela Sullivan
> William "Buddy" Sutton

Others:
Conrad and Joy Evans
Benjamin Hardy, Jr.
Ken Hechler
William Holloway, Jr.
James Hromas
Richard W. Poole
Jim Shideler
Jim Vallion

Other Resources

Derryberry, Bob, doctoral thesis on Robert Kerr, University of Missouri, August, 1973
Frontiers of Science Foundation Brochure and Report to the President, 1957

End Notes

Chapter One: Bennett

1. Family genealogical records loaned from Mrs. Norene Bryant, Nashville, Arkansas, November, 2005
2. Arkansas Secretary of State, www.sos.arkansas.gov/educational_history.html
3. Nevada County (Arkansas) Land Patents, 1888, page 20
4. Nevada County Courthouse, Prescott, Arkansas, "Marriages, Nevada County, Arkansas, 1871-1901," B-78
5. Family genealogical records loaned from Mrs. Norene Bryant, Nashville, Arkansas, November, 2005
6. *The Oklahoma A. & M. College Magazine*, February, 1952, Memorial Issue, page 5
7. Clark County Courthouse, Arkadelphia, Arkansas, Property Tax, 1880-1900, books, 16, 17 and 20
8. *The Ouachitonian*, 1915, Ouachita College, Arkadelphia, Arkansas, page 155
9. Personal interview with Thomas Edwin Bennett, Oklahoma City, Oklahoma, July 6, 2006
10. Truman Presidential Library, Oral Interviews, Liberty L. (Bennett) Preston, Mary L. (Bennett) Delozier and Mary B. (Delozier) Harris, Stillwater, Oklahoma, 1971 by Richard D. McKinzie, page 4
11. "HeritageQuest," database, Clark County, Arkansas, federal census of 1900, Southwestern Arkansas Regional Historical Society, Old Washington, Arkansas
12. *The Bearcat*, Ouachita College, 1907, Arkadelphia, Arkansas
13. Choctaw County Courthouse Teacher Employment Records, 1909-1910, Hugo, Oklahoma, page 3
14. Truman Presidential Library, Oral Interviews, Liberty L. (Bennett) Preston, Mary L. (Bennett) Delozier and Mary B. (Delozier) Harris, Stillwater, Oklahoma, 1971 by Richard D. McKinzie, page 35
15. "HeritageQuest," database, Bryan County, oklahoma, federal census of 1910, Southwestern Arkansas Regional Historical Society, Old Washington, Arkansas

16. *The Oklahoma A. & M. College Magazine*, February, 1952, Memorial Issue, page 6
17. *Southeastern Oklahoma State University Since 1909*, Volume 1, L. David Norris, 1986, page 131-132.
18. ibid., pages 139-149
19. *Governance, Centennial Histories Series*, James H. Boggs, Oklahoma State University Press, page 53
20. "Dr. Henry G. Bennett As I Knew Him," by Berlin B. Chapman, *Chronicles of Oklahoma*, Volume 33, 1955, pages 159-160
21. Research, Centennial Histories Series, Craig Chappell, Oklahoma State University Press, 1991, page 115
22. *The Oklahoma A. & M. College Magazine*, February, 1952, Memorial Issue, pages 8-9
23. Truman Presidential Library, Oral Interviews, Liberty L. (Bennett) Preston, Mary L. (Bennett) Delozier and Mary B. (Delozier) Harris, Stillwater, Oklahoma, 1971 by Richard D. McKinzie, page 64
24. *Oklahoma State University—Since 1890*, Philip Reed Rulon, 1975, page 262
25. Truman Presidential Library, Oral Interviews, Liberty L. (Bennett) Preston, Mary L. (Bennett) Delozier and Mary B. (Delozier) Harris, Stillwater, Oklahoma, 1971 by Richard D. McKinzie, page 92
26. Personal interview with Thomas Edwin Bennett, Oklahoma City, Oklahoma, July 6, 2006
27. Truman Presidential Archives, Henry Garland Bennett, Box #6, "Regional Council for Education"
28. *Stillwater News-Press*, September 10 and 13, 1945
29. Bennett family materials, letter from Department of Army, Richard C. O'Brien, Chief, Overseas Affairs Branch, February 14, 1949
30. ibid., Bennett Germany Report, August 24, 1949, six pages
31. ibid., cable from Mahateme Selassie, Vice Minister of Agriculture, Imperial Ethiopian Government, January 25, 1950
32. *A. & M. College Magazine*, June, 1950, pages 8-9
33. *The Buck Stops Here*, David M. Noyes and Edward J. Flynn, 2000, pages 79-80
34. Harry S. Truman Inaugural Speech, January 20, 1949, odur.let.reg.nl/-usa/P/ht33/speeches.Truman.html
35. *Counsel to the President*, Clark Clifford, 1991, pages 248-253
36. Truman Presidential Library Archives, Oral Interview, Stanley Andrews, October 31, 1970, page 14
37. Truman Presidential Library Archives, Oral Interview, Dr, Raymond W. Miller, October 13 and November 13, 1969, page 42
38. Personal Interview, Ken Hechler, Truman Presidential Library Archives, July 29, 2005

39. *The Daily Oklahoman*, November 14 and 15, 1950, page 1
40. *Stillwater News-Press*, November 22, 1950, page 1
41. *The Daily O'Collegian*, December 14, 1950
42. Truman Presidential Library Archives, Stanley Andrews, October 31, 1970, pages 30-32
43. *The Washington Post*, February 22, 1951, "Merry-Go-Round"
44. Bennett family materials, letter to Henry, Jr.; Phil and Tom Bennett, December 28, 1951, from Walker Stone, Editor of Scripps-Howard Newspaper Alliance, with copies of his editorial on Bennett
45. Vera Pearl Connell Bennett's personal diary of Central and South America travels, spring, 1951, donated to the Oklahoma History Center, Oklahoma City, Oklahoma
46. Truman Presidential Library Archives, Oral Interview, Christine Hardy Little, February 23, 1973, pages 31-32
47. *The Oklahoma A. &. M. College Magazine*, February, 1952, Memorial Issue, page 14
48. *The Pathfinder*, July, 1951, page 18
49. Bennett Family materials, Bennett speech in Minneapolis, Minnesota, November 28, 1951, donated to the International Education and Outreach Program, Oklahoma State University, Stillwater, Oklahoma
50. *Counsel to the President*, Clark Clifford, 1991, page 249
51. *Working With Truman*, Ken Hechler, 1982, pages 119-120
52. *The New York Times*, December 24, 1951, page 1
53. *The New York Herald Tribune*, December 24, 1951
54. *The Washington Post, December 24*, 1951
55. U. S. State Department Press Release 1111, December 23, 1951
56. Bennett family interviews
57. Presidential Statement December 23, 1951
58. U. S. State Department Press Release , December 29, 1951, Memorial Service at the State Department
59. *Stillwater News-Press*, "Senator Kerr's Text at Bennett Rites," January 10, 1952
60. *Daily Oklahoman*, "Final Bennett Services Held This Afternoon," January 8, 1952
61. *Stillwater News-Press*, "2,000 Attend Bennett Services," January 12, 1952
62. Bennett family materials, Walker Stone letter and editorials, December 28, 1951
63. Bennett family materials, U. S. State Department document, "Excerpts from the Message of the President on the State of the Union, Delivered to Congress on January 9, 1952"
64. Alemaya University, www.alemayau.edu.et
65. Oklahoma State University, www.okstate.edu

Chapter Two: Holloway

1. *Oklahoma's Governors, 1929-1955*, LeRoy Fischer, 1983, page 32
2. Ouachita Baptist University graduate records, Arkadelphia, Arkansas
3. Clark County Courthouse, Marriage Records, page 65
4. Personal interview with Tom Bennett, July, 2006, Oklahoma City, Oklahoma
5. *Arkansans of the Years*, "The Three Arkansas Musketeers," Fay Williams and C. C. Allards, 1952
6. *The Ouachitonian*, Ouachita College, 1910
7. *Oklahoma's Governors, 1929-1955*, LeRoy Fischer, 1983, page 32
8. Tom Bennett interview, OKC, July 6, 2006
9. *Oklahoma's Governors, 1929-1955*, LeRoy Fischer, 1983, page 32
10. ibid., page 33
11. ibid.
12. Oklahoma History Center, OKC, Governors' display
13. *Oklahoma's Governors, 1929-1955*, LeRoy Fischer, 1983, page 33
14. ibid.
15. "HeritageQuest," 1920 U. S. Census data
16. *Oklahoma's Governors, 1929-1955*, LeRoy Fischer, 1983, page 33
17. ibid.
18. ibid.
19. Oklahoma History Center, OKC, Governors' display
20. *Oklahoma's Governors, 1929-1955*, LeRoy Fischer, 1983, page 35
21. Truman Presidential Library, Oral interbiew, Liberty L. (Bennett) Preston, Mary L. (Bennett) Delozier and Mary B. (Delozier Harris. Stillwater, Oklahoma, 1971, by Richard D. McKinzie, page 48
22. *Oklahoma's Governors, 1929-1955*, LeRoy Fischer, 1983, page 35
23. ibid., page 36
24. Tom Bennett interview, OKC, July 6, 2006
25. *Oklahoma's Governors, 1929-1955*, LeRoy Fischer, 1983, page 37
26. ibid., pages 37-38
27. ibid., page 39
28. ibid.
29. Oklahoma Historical Society, Governor's speeches, page 6
30. ibid., page 8
31. *Oklahoma's Governors, 1929-1955*, LeRoy Fischer, 1983, page 47
32. ibid., page 43
33. ibid., page 44
34. ibid.
35. ibid., page 45
36. Personal Interview, Judge William Holloway, Jr., OKC, July, 2007
37. *Oklahoma's Governors, 1929-1955*, LeRoy Fischer, 1983, page 46

38. ibid.

39. ibid., page 49

40. Personal interview, Judge William Holloway, Jr., OKC, July, 2007

41. www.innsofcourt.org. "About Judge Holloway"

42. ibid.

43. Personal interview, Judge William Holloway, Jr., OKC, July 2007

44. www.innsofcourt.org. "About Judge Holloway

45. *The Oklahoma Times*, "Oklahoma, LBJ Pay tribute to Ex-Gov. W. J. Holloway," December 16, 1964

46. The Oklahoma History Center, Historical Archives Research, Holloway files, telegram from President Lyndon Baines Johnson

47. *Oklahoma's Governors, 1929-1955*, LeRoy Fischer, 1983, page 50

Chapter Three: Kerr

1. *Oklahoma's Governors, 1929-1955*, LeRoy Fischer, 1983, page 125

2. ibid.

3. ibid.

4. ibid.

5. ibid.

6. *American National Biography*, Volume 12, Garraty and Carnes, 1999, page 628

7. Derryberry, Bob, doctoral thesis on Robert Kerr, University of Missouri, August, 1973, page 25

8. ibid.

9. *American National Biography*, Volume 12, 1999, page 628

10. Derryberry, 1973, pages 25-26

11. *Oklahoma's Governors, 1929-1955*, LeRoy Fischer, 1983, page 126

12. ibid.

13. *American National Biography*, Volume 12, 1999, page 628

14. ibid.

15. *Oklahoma's Governors, 1929-1955*, LeRoy Fischer, 1983, page 126

16. ibid.

17. Derryberry, 1973, page 27

18. *Oklahoma's Governors, 1929-1955*, LeRoy Fischer, 1983, page 127

19. ibid.

20. ibid.

21. ibid. page 128

22. Derryberry, 1973, page 30

23. ibid.

24. *Oklahoma's Governors, 1929-1955*, LeRoy Fischer, 1983, page 129

25. ibid.

26. State of the State Address, Governor Robert Kerr, January 12, 1943, page 2

27. *Oklahoma's Governors, 1929-1955*, LeRoy Fischer, 1983, page 130
28. ibid., page 132
29. ibid., pages 132-133
30. ibid., page 133
31. Derryberry, 1973, page 34
32. *Oklahoma's Governors, 1929-1955*, LeRoy Fischer, 1983, page 134
33. ibid., page 135
34. ibid., page 136
35. ibid., page 138
36. Derryberry, 1973, page 36
37. *Oklahoma's Governors, 1929-1955*, LeRoy Fischer, 1983, page 138
38. ibid.
39. ibid., page 140
40. Derryberry, 1973, page 38
41. Bennett family materials, Frontiers of Science report brochures
42. *The Man Who Ran the Moon*, Piers Bizony, 2006, pages 14
43. *Oklahoma's Governors, 1929-1955*, LeRoy Fischer, 1983, page 143
44. ibid., page 144
45. *American National Biography, Volume 12*, 1999, page 629
46. ibid.
47. *The Buck Stops Here*, Noyes and Flynn, 2000,
48. *Truman*, David McCullough, 1992, page 844
49. *Stillwater News-Press*, Stillwater, Oklahoma, January 10, 1952
50. *Memoirs, Volume II*, Harry Truman, 1956, pages 557-558
51. *American National Biography, Volume 12*, 1999, page 629
52. *The Man Who Ran the Moon*, Piers Bixony, 2006, pages 15-16
53. *American National Biography, Volume 12*, 1999, page 629
54. Derryberry, 1973, page 42
55. Derryberry, 1973, page 48
56. *Oklahoma's Governors, 1929-1955*, LeRoy Fischer, 1983, page 145

Chapter Four: Truman

1. (www.pbs.org/AmericanExperience/ThePresidents)
2. ibid.
3. McCullough, David, *Truman*, 1992, pages 170-171
4. (www.worldwar1.com/tgws) "Captain Harry Truman, Artilleryman and Future President"
5. (www.pbs.org/AmericanExperience/ThePresidents)
6. McCullough, David, *Truman*, 1992, page 98
7. ibid., page 100
8. Truman Presidential Library, Oral interview, Liberty L. (Bennett) Preston, Mary L. (Bennett) Delozier and Mary B. (Delozier Harris. Stillwater, Oklahoma, 1971, by Richard D. McKinzie

9. (www.worldwarI.com/tgws) "Captain Harry Truman, Artilleryman and Future President"
10. Truman Presidential Library, President Calendar, Henry Bennett
11. Clifford, Clark, *Counsel to the President*, 1991, page 251
12. Bennett family personal materials
13. Truman Presidential Library, Oral interview, Liberty L. (Bennett) Preston, Mary L. (Bennett) Delozier and Mary B. (Delozier Harris. Stillwater, Oklahoma, 1971, by Richard D. McKinzie
14. Truman Presidential Library, President Calendar, Henry Bennett
15. *Stillwater News-Press*, November 15, 1950
16. Ferrell, Robert, *The Private Papers of Harry S. Truman*, 1980, page 234
17. Truman Presidential Library, President Calendar, Henry Bennett
18. ibid.
19. McCullough, David, *Truman*, 1992, page 848
20. ibid., pages 810-812
21. ibid., pages 826-827
22. ibid., pages 827-829
23. Truman Presidential Library, Oral Interviews, Stanley Andrews, 1970
24. Hechler, Ken, *Working with Truman*, 1982, page 283
25. McCullough, *Truman*, 1992, pages 989-990
26. ibid., page 991
27. Ferrell, Robert, *Truman, A Century of Remembrance*, 1984, page 249

Chapter Five: Selassie
1. *Encyclopedia of World Biography, Volume 7*, "Haile Selaissie," page 68
2. *Current Biography*, 1954, "Haile Selassie," pages 315-316
3. Marcus, *Haile Selassie I: The Formative Years, 1892-1936*, 1987
4. *Kings and Queens*, page 157
5. *Current Biography*, 1954, page 316
6. ibid.
7. www.boomshaka/league.html
8. *Current Biography*, 1954, page 316
9. ibid.
10. ibid., page 317
11. Gill, Jerry, *International Programs*, Oklahoma State University, 1991, page 7
12. ibid., page 9
13. ibid., page 12
14. ibid., page 13
15. ibid., page 14
16. ibid., pages 15-16
17. ibid., page 22

18. ibid.
19. ibid., page 46
20. ibid., page 48
21. ibid., page 51
22. Bennett family materials and interviews
23. ibid.
24. ibid.
25. Gill, Jerry, *International Programs*, Oklahoma State University, 1991, page 55
26. ibid., page 29
27. ibid., page 59
28. ibid.
29. ibid.
30. *Encyclopedia of World Biography, Volume 7*, page 69
31. ibid.
32. (www.cnn.com) 2001
33. ibid.
34. ibid.
35. ibid.
36. Personal interview with Joy and Conrad Evans, 2008, Stillwater, Oklahoma
37. ibid.
38. ibid.
39. ibid.
40. Gill, Jerry, *International Programs*, Oklahoma State University, 1991, page 33
41. Personal interviews with Joy and Conrad Evans, 2008
42. (www.ieo.okstate.edu)
43. ibid.
44. ibid.
45. ibid.
46. ibid.

Chapter Six: Hardy

1. Truman Presidential Library, Oral Interview, Christine Hardy Little, Arlington, Virginia, 1973, Richard D. McKinzie, sections 1-2
2. ibid., section 3
3. ibid., section 4
4. ibid., section 5
5. ibid.
6. ibid., sections 7-8
7. ibid., section 9
8. ibid., section 11

9. ibid., section 12
10. ibid., sections 13-14
11. ibid., section 11
12. ibid., section 16
13. ibid., section 17
14. ibid., section 18
15. War on Hunger, A Report from the Agency for International Development, "Point IV," May, 1973
16. Clifford, Clark, *Counsel to the President*, 1991, page 250
17. Truman Presidential Library, Oral Interview, Christine Hardy Little, Arlington, Virginia, 1973, Richard D. McKinzie, section 20
18. War on Hunger, A Report from the Agency for International Development, "Point IV," May, 1973
19. ibid.
20. Truman Presidential Library, Archive speeches
21. Truman Presidential Library, Oral Interview, Christine Hardy Little, Arlington, Virginia, 1973, Richard D. McKinzie, section 23
22. ibid.
23. Foreign Service Journal, April, 1969
24. Elsey, George, *An Unexplained Life*, 2005, page 175
25. Clifford, Clark, *Counsel to the President*, 1991, page 249
26. Bennett Family materials, donated to the International Education and Outreach Program of Oklahoma State University
27. Hardy family materials, letter from Ben Hardy to Mr. Jonathan Daniels, Raleigh, North Carolina, November 19, 1950
28. War on Hunger, A Report from the Agency for International Development, "Point IV," May, 1973
29. ibid.
30. Hardy family materials, letter from Ben Hardy to Mr. Jonathan Daniels, Raleigh, North Carolina, November 19, 1950
31. Speech Release, USAID, January 20, 1999
32. War on Hunger, A Report from the Agency for International Development, "Point IV," May, 1973
33. Speech Release, USAID, January 20, 1999
34. Bennett family materials, Mrs. Bennett's personal travel diary, donated to the Oklahoma History Center, Oklahoma City, Oklahoma
35. Truman Presidential Library, Oral Interview, Christine Hardy Little, Arlington, Virginia, 1973, Richard D. McKinzie, section 32
36. Bennett family materials, Mrs. Bennett's personal travel diary, donated to the Oklahoma History Center, Oklahoma City, Oklahoma
37. Hardy family materials, letter from Ben Hardy to Mr. Jonathan Daniels, Raleigh, North Carolina, November 19, 1950
38. Bennett Family materials, donated to the International Education and Out-

reach Program of Oklahoma State University
39. Truman Presidential Library, Video archives, Point Four travel script
40. Truman Presidential Library, Oral Interview, Stanley Andrews, section 19
41. Truman Presidential Library, Video archives, Point Four travel script
42. Bennett Family materials, donated to the International Education and Outreach Program of Oklahoma State University
43. Correspondence with Benjamin Hardy, III, 2008
44. Truman Presidential Library, Oral Interview, Christine Hardy Little, Arlington, Virginia, 1973, Richard D. McKinzie, section 28-29
45. Truman Presidential Library, Archives, Hardy papers
46. Speech Release, USAID, January 20, 1999
47. ibid.

Chapter Seven: Webb

1. Lambright, W. Henry, *Powering Apollo*, 1995, page 11
2. ibid., page 14
3. Piers, Bizony, *The Man Who Ran the Moon,* 2006, page 9
4. Lambright, W. Henry, *Powering Apollo*, 1995, page 16
5. ibid., page 17
6. ibid., pages 19-20
7. ibid., page 22
8. ibid., page 23
9. ibid.
10. Piers, Bizony, *The Man Who Ran the Moon*, 2006, page 11
11. Lambright, W. Henry, *Powering Apollo*, 1995, page 30
12. *American National Biography*, Volume 22, 1999, page 849
13. Lambright, W. Henry, *Powering Apollo*, 1995, page 31
14. ibid., page 34
15. ibid., page 38
16. ibid., page 41
17. ibid., page 42
18. Truman Presidential Library, Oral Interview, James Webb, February 20, 1980, section 42
19. Lambright, W. Henry, *Powering Apollo*, 1995, page 40
20. ibid., page 45
21. ibid., page 47
22. ibid.
23. ibid.
24. Truman Presidential Library, Oral Interview, James Webb, February 20, 1980, section 43
25. Lambright, W. Henry, *Powering Apollo*, 1995, page 55
26. Truman Presidential Library, Hardy Papers, speech copy, June, 1949

27. McCullough, *Truman*, 1992, page 776
28. Lambright, W. Henry, *Powering Apollo*, 1995, page 60
29. Bennett Family materials, donated to the International Education and Outreach Program of Oklahoma State University
30. Bennett Family materials, donated to the International Education and Outreach Program of Oklahoma State University, U. S. State Department document released, January 11, 1952
31. *American National Biography*, Volume 22, 1999, page 849
32. ibid.
33. Bennett family materials, donated to the Oklahoma History Center, Oklahoma City, Oklahoma, Frontiers of Science Foundation brochure
34. ibid.
35. Bennett family materials, donated to the Oklahoma History Center, Oklahoma City, Oklahoma, Frontiers of Science Foundation "Report to the President,"
36. ibid.
37. ibid.
38. ibid.
39. *Oklahoma City Times*, "Attorney Gets Oil Equipment Executive Job," April 4, 1956
40. Piers, Bizony, *The Man Who Ran the Moon*, 2006, page 15-17
41. ibid., page 17
42. Lambright, W. Henry, *Powering Apollo*, 1995, page 82
43. The Bureaucrat, Professional Leaders Series, "James E. Webb and NASA," Summer, 1986, page 16
44. Lambright, W. Henry, *Powering Apollo*, 1995, page 87
45. The Bureaucrat, Professional Leaders Series, "James E. Webb and NASA," Summer, 1986, page 17
46. Lambright, W. Henry, *Powering Apollo*, 1995, page 96
47. ibid., pages 96-97
48. ibid., page 101
49. *American National Biography*, Volume 22, 1999, page 849
50. ibid.
51. *The Gannetteer*, "James E. Webb: Space Age's Incredible Leader," October, 1974
52. Lambright, W. Henry, *Powering Apollo*, 1995, page 91
53. ibid., page 99
54. ibid., page 103
55. *American National Biography*, Volume 22, 1999, page 849
56. Lambright, W. Henry, *Powering Apollo*, 1995, page 147
57. Piers, Bizony, *The Man Who Ran the Moon*, 2006, page 119
58. ibid., page 177
59. Lambright, W. Henry, *Powering Apollo*, 1995, page 201

60. ibid., page 204
61. *The Gannetteer*, "James E. Webb: Space Age's Incredible Leader," October, 1974
62. *Wall Street Journal*, "NASA's Jim Webb—a Rare Bureaucrat," October 11, 1968
63. *American National Biography*, Volume 22, 1999, page 850
64. Lambright, W. Henry, *Powering Apollo*, 1995, page 5
65. *American National Biography*, Volume 22, 1999, page 850
66. Piers, Bizony, *The Man Who Ran the Moon*, 2006, page 205
67. *Wall Street Journal*, "NASA's Jim Webb—a Rare Bureaucrat," October 11, 1968
68. Personal interview with Dr. Richard Poole, 2007, Oklahoma City, Oklahoma
69. Lambright, W. Henry, *Powering Apollo*, 1995, page 211
70. ibid.
71. Piers, Bizony, *The Man Who Ran the Moon*, 2006, page 203
72. ibid., page 212
73. ibid., page 213
74. ibid., page 216
75. www.jwst.nasa.gov

Index

O

O'Brien, Richard C., 8
O'Keefe, Sean, 94
Oklahoma A and M
    College, 5, 8, 24, 26,
    41
Oklahoma Baptist
    University, 34, 36
Oklahoma City oil basin,
    35, 86
Oklahoma History
    Center, 20
Oklahoma State Univer-
    sity (OSU), 20, 87
Henry G. Bennett
    Distinguished
    Fellow Award, 65
Henry G. Bennett
    Distinguished
    Service Award, 20
International Education
    and Outreach
    Program (OSUIEO),
    20, 64
School of International
    Studies (SIS), 64
Otjen, William J., 36
Organization for African
    Unity, 62
Ouachita College (Baptist
    University), 2, 3, 7,
    21, 22, 23, 28

P

Paine, Thomas, 91, 92
Peace Corps, 19
Phillips, Leon C., 35, 36,
    38
Point Four, 8, 10, 11, 12,
    13, 14, 15, 17, 18,
    19, 20, 30, 43, 50,
    51, 52, 58, 59,
    60,62, 63, 64, 65,
    69, 70, 71, 72, 73,
    74, 75, 76, 77, 83,
    84, 85, 86

Poole, Richard W., 87, 93
Pou, Edward W., 80

Q

Quebec International
    Food and Agricul-
    tural Organization,
    8, 15, 58

R

Reconstruction Finace
    Corporation, 43
Republic Supply
    Company, 87
Rizley, Ross, 40
Rockefeller, Nelson, 51
Roosevelt, Mrs. Eleanor,
    19
Roosevelt, Franklin D.,
    35, 80
Ross, Charlie, 52
Rotary International, 4
Rusk, Dean, 85
Russell, Francis, 69, 70,
    71, 77

S

Sandmeyer, Robert, 64
Selassie, Haile, 8, 47
Servico, 11
Shelton, Reba, 34-35
Shepherd, Alan, 88
Smith, Gomer, 36, 40
Smithsonian Institute, 93,
    94
Southeastern State
    Normal School
    (SEN), 3
Southeastern State
    Teachers College
    (STC), 4
Sperry Gyroscope
    Company, 80
Stigler, William G., 39
Stassen, Harold, 60
Stone, Walker, 18, 19

T

Technical Cooperation
    Agency (TCA), 11,
    59, 60, 73
"Town and Gown," 3
Toynbee, Arnold, 77
"Trizonia," 8
Truman, John, 45
Truman, Harry S., 9, 10,
    11, 12, 14, 17, 19,
    39, 40, 41, 42, 45-
    54, 70, 74, 77, 81,
    82, 83, 84, 85, 90
Truman, Margaret, 45
"Twenty-five Year Plan,"
    5

U

United Nations, 9, 85
U. S. Agency for
    International
    Development
    (USAID), 19, 77
U. S. Budget Bureau, 13,
    49, 81, 84, 89
U. S. Department of
    Agriculture (USDA),
    8, 11, 13, 51, 63
U. S. Department of
    Defense, 84, 89, 92
U. S. Department of the
    Interior, 11, 13, 51
U. S. Department of
    Public Health, 51
U. S. Department of
    State, 10, 11, 12, 13,
    14, 17, 19, 49, 50,
    51, 68, 69, 70,
    71,72, 76, 83, 84,
    85, 86, 89
U. S. Department of
    Treasury, 13, 51

W

Wall Street Crash, 27
Wallace, Bess, 47, 48
Watkins, Wes, 20, 64
Webb, Gorham, 81
Webb, James Edwin, 9,
    10, 17, 41, 43, 47,
    49, 50, 51, 53, 74,
    79-94
Webb, Jr., James Edwin,
    81

Webb, John Frederick, 79
Webb, Sarah Gorham, 79
Wentz, Louis (Lew)
    Haynes, 25
White, Edward, 90
Wilham, Oliver S., 59, 64
Women Accepted for
    Volunteer Emergency
    Service (WAVES), 6
World War I, 23, 34, 46,
    47, 79

World War II, 5, 8, 9, 12,
    30, 37, 41, 57, 68,
    80, 81, 83

Y

Yasu, Lij

Z

Zauditu, Empress

1870870

Made in the USA